# What Color Is Your Dog?

# What Color Is Your Dog?

## TRAIN YOUR DOG BASED ON HIS PERSONALITY "COLOR"

By

## Joel Silverman

Kennel Club Books®
A Division of BowTie, Inc.

## Kennel Club Books®

**A Division of BowTie, Inc.**

40 Broad Street
Freehold, NJ 07728 • USA
www.kennelclubbooks.com

Library of Congress Cataloging-in-Publication Data

Silverman, Joel, 1958-
   What color is your dog? : train your dog based on his
personality "color" / by Joel Silverman.
      p. cm.
   ISBN 978-1-59378-645-8
   1. Dogs—Behavior. 2. Dogs—Training. I. Title.
   SF433.S59 2008
   636.7'0887—dc22

                                                2008043796

Printed and bound in USA
16  15 14  13  12  11  10  09      1  2  3  4  5  6  7  8  9 10

# CONTENTS

# FOREWORD

I first met Joel Silverman on the set of our TV show *Drs. Foster and Smith Faithful Friends*. Joel was one of the expert guests we had invited to be on the show to demonstrate dog-training techniques. Joel's way with animals and his explanations immediately attracted my attention. I liked his approach.

As a veterinarian and an animal lover, I have always owned and trained dogs. And for nearly three decades, I've helped organize seminars to help others learn how to train man's best friend to do his tasks well while enjoying them, too. That was why I was immediately attracted to Joel's way around his dogs. His dogs were obedient, yes, but it was clear that they were obedient because they wanted to be. They were having fun with Joel! That is how it is supposed to work. The relationship between a dog and his owner can and should be a fun one, where each knows his role and enjoys it.

Not every dog owner has that experience, however. Just like people, dogs have different personalities. Working in veterinary medicine all of my adult life allowed me to see those personality differences firsthand. If a dog owner doesn't understand a dog's personality and how that particular dog learns best, the result is all too often an unhappy owner and an unhappy dog. Joel's system of identifying a dog's personality by answering the question "What color is your dog?" is a great leap forward in helping dogs and their owners develop great relationships—and in helping dog owners train their faithful friends in the way in which they will learn best.

Joel first described this system to me while we were shooting the second season of *Faithful Friends*. As I heard him describe the concept of *What Color Is Your Dog?* I was immediately intrigued and asked about reading the book. I'm glad I did. You'll be glad you read this book, too.

In *What Color Is Your Dog?* Joel outlines for you how to easily identify your dog's personality type using five different categories, each assigned a different color. Characteristics of each color category are explained, along with training techniques and how various tools are used for each one. In each color category he explains how to teach the basic commands *come, sit, stay,* and *no.* Tips are provided so you as a trainer will know how to respond to your dog's personality and reactions.

Joel's system makes training so simple that even an old vet like me could do it! I wish I had recognized this method forty years ago!

Get ready for a great read, and a great time with your faithful friend as a result.

Dr. Marty Smith
*Drs. Foster and Smith Pet Supplies*

# INTRODUCTION

One of the biggest mistakes that a dog owner or a trainer can make is to think that all dogs should be trained in exactly the same way, using the same technique. Why? Because dogs are individuals, each with his own fascinating and definitive personality. Some are the fiery sort, easily sent into a barking, tail-wagging frenzy. Others possess a mellower disposition—laid-back and ready to go with your flow. Then there are the shy ones, the timid ones, the closet refugees. The training techniques that work fine with a shy dog (what I call a Blue dog), that help him build confidence and energize him, can fail miserably with a fiery dog (a Red dog), stirring him up and making him harder to control. That is hardly surprising when you consider the real difference in the dogs' personalities.

It is essential that new dog owners and trainers take the opportunity to get to know their dogs, understand what types of dogs they are dealing with, and train their dogs based on those personalities. I hope to help you do just that with *What Color Is Your Dog?* In this book, I have divided dogs' personalities into five general groups: Red, Orange, Yellow, Green, and Blue. My training suggestions correspond to each color, as each one has its own unique styles, techniques, and methods.

Before I explain my system further, I want to emphasize again that if you have not done so already, you must take time, before training begins, to develop a relationship with your dog. You must *know* the animal you are working with before you can effectively teach him. Many dog owners have made the mistake of taking a dog straight from an animal shelter, humane society, or breeder into training, without bonding with him first. When this occurs, the animal is often forced into an uncomfortable, even frightening, situation. Depending on the animal's personality, the outcome can be disastrous. A shy or timid dog can become afraid and possibly turn into a "fear biter." A slightly aggressive dog can become truly aggressive. Unfortunately, too many dogs get returned to breeders, shelters, and rescue societies because their owners have decided they are "untrainable"— when in reality the fault lies with the people, who did not bond with their pets and learn about their personalities before trying to train them. The best animal trainers I have ever been around were the ones who got to know the animal they were training, became the animal's friend, and built trust.

For the past thirty years, I've been teaching people about dog training and responsible pet ownership, all the while looking for new ways to make the training and care of a dog easier and more enjoyable for the average owner. In examining the techniques I've used and messages I've delivered, I find that the two points I outlined above stand out: one, that people need to develop relationships with their dogs before training them; and two, that dogs, like people, have a wide variety of personalities and should be trained accordingly.

In *What Color Is Your Dog?* you'll find training suggestions geared specifically to the personality of your dog. So to use the book, you'll first need to determine the "color" of your dog. Is he an extremely high-strung Red? Or just a slightly jumpy Orange? Could he be a middle-of-the-road, changeable Yellow? Or is he a somewhat shy and withdrawn Green? Then again, perhaps he is an incredibly intimidated and fearful Blue? (These, of course, are only a few of the ways to describe the dogs that fall into the five personality groups. You will find more in-depth descriptions in chapter 1.)

It is important to understand that these color designations are based on a dog's personality. I want to emphasize that point because a colleague recently drew my attention to a very different color system. In a 1997 article in *Off-Lead Magazine,*

"The Color of Dog Training," Colleen McDaniel discussed the dog's as well as the owner's constantly changing states of mind, which she said could run the gamut from blue to red (calm state to excited state) in a single day—like a mood ring! My color concept is based in the dog's actual temperament, not a passing mood.

Once you identify the color of your dog, you can go to the corresponding chapter for the appropriate teaching style. I will help you teach your dog three new behaviors—*sit*, *stay*, *come*—and the word *no*, which I believe are essential for all dogs to know and understand.

Your dog needs to know how to *sit* and *stay* because if you have the front door opened, you must be confident that your dog will sit and stay there, not run out. It is an excellent, essential, and easy form of control and communication for all dog owners. Your dog needs to know how to *come*, so that if your dog does run out the door or is distracted, you will have the control of knowing that the dog will come back to you. Finally, your dog must understand the word *no* because it is the best way to communicate to him that what he is doing at that instant is unacceptable. As you will learn later in this book, animals are very much like people. Simply put, children need to understand the word *no* and so do dogs.

Each chapter in the training portion of the book is separated into five areas: Red, Orange, Yellow, Green, and Blue. The great news is that although in this book there are five ways to train, *you will only need to use one.*

I hope you will not only learn a lot but also have a lot of fun at the same time.

Good luck!

# What Color *Is* Your Dog?

**E**very dog, like every person, has his own, unique personality. A fuzzy, burrowing new litter of Golden Retrievers, for example, may have just been birthed by the same dam, but no two siblings are exactly alike in disposition. Every single one of them wants warmth and nourishment, but one little guy in the center of the pack may be kicking up a great fuss about the whole situation while his brother to the left lies calmly awaiting future events. The difference between the two? The kicker is an Orange puppy; the mellow one is a Yellow puppy.

The colors, of course, don't refer to their coats, but to their personality types: I developed this color-coding system as a way of helping you classify your dog for training purposes. As you train your dog

# DEVELOPING A RELATIONSHIP

By incorporating my Companions for Life system of training, you will address that first and most important step: developing a relationship with your dog. There are three stages:

## 1. GETTING TO KNOW YOUR DOG

All successful trainers agree that a relationship needs to be established before it can grow and that trainers must get to know the animals they will be training. Even in working with marine mammals such as killer whales and dolphins, I found it essential to know each individual I was training.

A good trainer will always take the time to learn everything possible about the animal and will find a way to motivate the animal to *want to be around the trainer.* Once you identify some things that stimulate the animal, give the animal those certain things at the most opportune times.

## 2. DEVELOPING A RELATIONSHIP

I have continued training animals over the past thirty years for many reasons—the biggest being that it is a lot of fun. When it's fun for the animal, when he's really into it, the enjoyment is multiplied. I've also been in situations early in my career where I've seen what happens when a relationship was *never* developed and the animal *was not* having fun. The training session could quickly go south as it turned into a boring and unpleasant experience for everyone involved.

## 3. BUILDING TRUST

Years ago, as I started to build my training system, the one idea that always remained a key factor was getting animals to want to work with me. But for that to happen, I found that I first needed to develop the trust. The valuable lesson I learned was that to establish trust, I needed to simply get to know the animal, develop a relationship, and become his friend. The animal needed to know I had his best interests at heart at all times. This created something awesome: a desire for the animal to want to learn.

One of the best ways to understand building trust is to understand what trust really means. In the animal world, this means the animal now feels safe allowing us to feed him, give him water, love him, play with him, keep him sheltered, and be his friend. Most important, this lays the groundwork to make the training process easier, more efficient, and much more fun.

in the coming weeks, you will find that the technique you will use from this book will be based on your dog's specific personality.

The two central aspects of my training philosophy are the need to develop a relationship with your dog (see "Developing a Relationship" on the opposite page) and the importance of training dogs differently according to their individual personalities—or, as I designate them here, their colors, Red, Orange, Yellow, Green, and Blue.

Why have you not heard more about the importance of personalities in training? I think simply because many dog trainers tend to generalize and give the pet owner one way to train a specific behavior. They will tell you to put a leash and collar on your dog and away you go. Unfortunately, that doesn't always work; in fact, the results can be devastating for the dog.

## DETERMINING YOUR DOG'S COLOR

Where in our five-color scheme does your dog fall? It is time to put him to the test so that you'll be able to utilize the right training materials in the book. Take a look at "Let the

Here are some questions you want to ask yourself to help assess your dog's personality.

### If you have a dog that is out of control:

- Is your dog a little high-strung—or maybe even *very* high-strung?
- Does he constantly jump on people?
- Does he bark and get out of control when you come home?
- Does he pull hard on the leash when you walk him?
- Is there a little aggression in your dog, or is your dog's breed considered aggressive?
- Does your dog express a natural prey drive? (This means an instinct to want to chase animals.)

If your dog has any of these characteristics to the *extreme*, your dog is most likely a *Red* dog. If your dog displays some of these characteristics, but to a lesser degree, your dog is most likely an *Orange* dog.

### If you think your dog is shy or timid:

- Is your dog afraid of older people, men, women, or people in uniform?
- Is your dog afraid of other animals?
- Does he get nervous when you correct him or simply say the word *no*?
- Does your dog try to run away?
- Is your dog naturally nervous, or does he shake sometimes?

If your dog has any of these characteristics to the *extreme*, he is most likely a *Blue* dog. If your dog displays several of these characteristics, but not to the extreme of a Blue dog, your dog is most likely a *Green* dog.

If your dog does not seem to have any of these characteristics to any discernable degree, then he is most likely a Yellow dog. Congratulations! Your training sessions should be much easier than they would be with any other color dog.

Assessment Begin!" (opposite page), and read the following descriptions on each of the color (personality) groups.

Let's start off with the Yellow dog, sitting squarely in the center of our spectrum. The Yellow dog, with his naturally laid-back personality, can prove very easy to train. Why? Because of his "mellow yellow" nature, your dog's personality will most likely be determined by your own actions and attitudes.

Think about the people you know who are very easy-going. They tend to just go with the flow. If you're happy and excited, so is a mellow person; if you are more placid, so is he or she. The same thing applies to your relationship with a Yellow dog. A firm, in-control voice and mannerisms will calm the dog. A more outgoing and excited approach will quickly increase the dog's excitement level. As you will see, this "mirroring" of your attitude can play an important role in training.

Look at the outer colors in our spectrum: the Blue dogs and the Red dogs. A Blue dog will probably be quite shy and possess some sort of fear. As with a shy or timid person, you need to be a little more patient when you interact with a Blue dog. On the other end of the spectrum, we have the Red dog. A Red dog is totally out of control, off the wall, and hyperactive. People who are incredibly outgoing, wound up, and boisterous are easily excitable, aren't they? You will find that it takes more effort to convince them to focus on the matter at hand. The same thing applies to the Red dog.

If you assess the personalities of Red and Blue dogs, they could not be less alike. Because the dogs are very different, it makes sense that the training techniques you use with them will be, too. As you read this book, you will learn that the way you touch, talk to, and train a Blue dog can be 100 percent different from the way you touch, talk to, and train a Red dog.

Here is something to keep in mind: never base your determination of your dog's color/personality on his breed. Although certain breeds may tend to be predominantly one end of the spectrum than another when born, that doesn't mean all dogs in that breed will have those initial personalities. For example, although Labs might be some degree of Red or Orange at birth, there may be a Yellow or Green puppy or two in each litter. Would it be a common thing to see a litter of Labs that are all Yellows or Greens? No, but from time to time you will encounter Labs with those personality types.

Later in this book, you'll find the special chapter that teaches you the best training methods for dogs that share your dog's color. To get you started, here is a little information on the five vibrant shades of canine personality.

## Red Dogs

To reiterate, these are high-strung dogs or dogs with very outgoing personalities. The personalities of Red dogs vary widely. The dogs that exhibit these personality traits could also range in every size and breed, from a small Parson Russell Terrier to a large Labrador Retriever.

Because an Extremely Red dog is likely to be very difficult to control, you will face most of the challenges or problems

This dog's high-energy excitement tells us without a doubt that he is a Red dog.

## PORTRAIT OF A RED DOG

Years back, I found an incredible Red dog for an IAMS commercial. Not that I was initially thrilled about using an amateur (in the entertainment world) dog on that end of the spectrum. After all, even bringing an edgy and inexperienced Orange dog to the set could be a little disconcerting; bringing a high-strung Red dog could be downright nerve wracking. But this commercial, with its energetic running shots, called for a Red. Fortunately, I discovered a team of liver Brittany Spaniels that were field champions. They were trained to work with people on horseback and were the top dogs at it.

The training for the lead dog, Flash, proved to be intense, because we needed to teach this Red dog to calm down. The running shots were not a problem, of course, but there were also the tougher shots, the ones requiring more control, such as standing still and barking on cue. In the end, Flash did a great job. A lot of the success came from our knowing how to train a Red dog properly and understanding that in fact he wanted to work and just needed to be given a job. By that I mean that he needed a focus for all that energy. We channeled that drive in the direction of *learning control* and ended up with a great dog for the commercial.

at the beginning of training. The initial training period will require much patience, but this patience will pay large dividends in later stages.

When dealing with a Red dog, you should avoid actions that will increase his arousal further or animate him. Because high energy and upbeat personalities characterize Red dogs, you will want to be just the opposite when you train them. You will do things that require a lot of control on your part because your dog is probably not going to want to stay in one place.

The metaphor I like to use is that the person training a Red dog should serve as *an anchor on a boat*. A strong, swift current may toss the boat about a bit, but the vessel will not spin away, totally out of control, if the anchor is heavy enough.

Your tone of voice is also key. If you have a lot of excitement in your voice, it stands to reason that the sound will excite your Red dog, too. Always strive to remain stable and in control, like that anchor. It is essential that you are always clear and very direct with Red dogs; they do not grasp subtleties well.

I have found that introducing food or treats as a component of training Red dogs can intensify their excitability. *Avoiding the use of food rewards when training this type of dog is probably one of the biggest differences between my technique and other positive training methods.* Instead of using treats to reinforce the behavior of Red dogs, I recommend using tactile rewards, such as petting the dogs and giving them special attention.

## Orange Dogs

Like Red dogs, Orange dogs have lots of personality. However, they do not approach the intensity of the Red dog—think of them as Reds turned down a notch. Orange dogs exhibit a range of personalities. The size of the dog is

As with a Red dog, you need to be an anchor for an Orange dog.

## PORTRAIT OF AN ORANGE DOG

If you ever watched any of the *Empty Nest* episodes (the TV show aired 1988–1995) and looked carefully, you might have occasionally seen a slightly different-looking dog playing Dreyfuss, the family pet (usually played by the dog Bear). The impostor was Julio, Bear's brother. The big difference between them was in personality. While Bear was an Orange dog turned Yellow through training, Julio sank his teeth into his Orangeness and refused to let go.

I had the opportunity to train Bear and Julio on *Empty Nest* from 1988 to 1992. When we started the show, Bear was a very playful one-year-old Orange dog. He is a great example of how constant exposure and working can make a dog move toward the center of the spectrum.

Julio was basically trained to do a lot of what Bear did, but unlike Bear, every move that he made looked too deliberate. One of the challenges of working with an Orange dog on a set is that sometimes things do not look natural. For example, you can give a dog a simple cue to "lie down" and follow it with a "head down." With a Yellow dog such as Bear, the response to those two cues would be very slow and natural movements. But an Orange Dog such as Julio would plop body and head down immediately, making it clear that he was obeying a command rather than appearing to lie down on his own (acting, you could say). This is why Julio was used so seldom and only for shots in which we wanted the dog to seem a bit "dramatic."

Another Orange stand-in was Bear's son Banjo—shown with Bear (left) and me in the photo above.

immaterial, ranging from a handful of Chihuahua to a barrelful of German Shepherd Dog. An Orange dog that leans toward Yellow will be a lot of fun to train right from the beginning. Training an Orange dog that leans toward Red may present more challenges.

As with the Red dog, the anchor principle applies. As the weighty anchor, you can steady the boat—your Orange dog—even in rough waters. With Orange dogs leaning toward Red, you should initially follow the same recommendations I gave for Red dogs: Avoid anything that stimulates his excitement, such as treats. Use the tactile reward system combined with a calm, soothing voice.

An Orange dog that leans toward Yellow will be a little different. You may be able to introduce treats as an aspect of training from the beginning, without the dog's losing control. The ability to use food as a reward will, of course, make things easier in the long run because food is one of the greatest forms of motivation.

## Yellow Dogs

Because they lack the extreme characteristics of Blue and Red dogs, "middle-of-the-road" Yellow dogs are more fun and easier to train from the outset. As mentioned earlier in the chapter, the changeable nature of the mellow Yellow is largely dictated by your actions—excited at certain times, calm at others—and the context of the training.

The best training techniques will vary depending on the individual characteristics of *your* Yellow companion. There is really a luxury in having the opportunity to train Yellow dogs because you can employ a variety of techniques, some

**Thanks to the time and love of his excellent owner, this pit bull mix turned from an Orange dog into a Yellow dog.**

## PORTRAIT OF A YELLOW DOG

In much of this book, I talk about dogs starting at a certain color and moving toward the center of the spectrum. But sometimes you might be lucky enough to find a dog that is naturally Yellow. That was the case with Duke (a dog I miss every day). I actually adopted him from the North County Humane Society in Oceanside, California. A great example of Duke's Yellowness is that when all the other dogs in the shelter were barking, he was just lying there, relaxed as can be, watching them all.

Duke was the German Shepherd mix that you see in the Companions for Life logo. Duke was easy to train because of his biddable, easygoing nature, and he became a true animal star. He appeared in more than sixty commercials. One was a Polaroid commercial in which the dog is blamed for going into the trash; he exonerates himself by snapping a picture of the true culprit, the family cat. Another was a Nissan commercial aired during the Super Bowl in which Duke hypnotizes his owner and picks up all the other dogs in the car, eventually leaving the owner in the street.

It was great using Duke on this shoot because there were times the crew needed him to stay in the driver's seat for a few hours while they were lighting shots. Only a mellow Yellow dog such as Duke would have put up with that.

from the cool side and some from the warm side of the spectrum. For those times when you want to rev up his excitement level, you can utilize the techniques most frequently used in the training of Blue dogs and Green dogs. For those times when you want to calm your dog and gain a little more control, you can rely on techniques used for Red dogs and Orange dogs. A Yellow dog will most often look to you for guidance.

One of the great aspects about training Yellow dogs is that you can offer them a variety of rewards with equally good results.

## Green Dogs

Green dogs, which may move more slowly than Red or Orange dogs, are somewhat shy or slightly fearful. That fearfulness may be the result of having been poorly cared for, improperly trained, abused, or exposed to frightening situations. If your Green dog is in any way withdrawn or scares easily, you will probably need to address some behavioral issues during the training process.

With the Green dog, remember that we are now moving toward the opposite end of the spectrum from the Red dog (and away from that nice, malleable Yellow), so the training is going to look much different. Be aware, also, that *degrees* of Green dogs exist. A shy and fearful dog has a tendency toward the Blue end of the personality spectrum; a less reserved dog might lean toward Yellow. As with Orange dogs, when you begin to train a Green dog that leans toward Yellow, the process will be much easier.

His tucked tail and wary behavior clearly show that this little Green dog needs a great deal of time and patience.

## PORTRAIT OF A GREEN DOG

I wanted to include this dog because so many people tell me that they have a dog that is Green-Orange. If you look at the color spectrum, Green is nowhere near Orange. But I know they are probably talking about a dog like Pulse. I had a chance to work with this dog, a McNab (a shorthaired Border Collie), and her trainer on an IAMS commercial shoot.

The most interesting thing is that although Pulse was cast for this job based on her athletic ability and her energy level, she is a Green dog. That means she can be very apprehensive toward people and unfamiliar situations, and it is this characteristic that marks her as a Green dog. At the same time, this breed of dog is incredibly athletic. Border Collies can really move fast when you are training them, once they have the opportunity to get comfortable.

I saw a great example of the dog's Green side one day when we were shooting. A squirrel had jumped in a tree overhead, and the dog was totally fixated on the critter. We had to stop everything until we got the squirrel out of the tree. The trainer took her time and waited for Pulse to get refocused on work. If a less knowledgeable trainer had tried to force Pulse, a Green dog, back to work, she might have gotten a little shyer (a little Greener), and we might have had problems.

When you are assessing your dog, make sure that you take a close look at his *natural* personality and not whether he is athletic. Your dog's natural personality, not his athleticism, will indicate his color.

It is imperative in training Green dogs that you find a way to get the dog interested in you. Unlike in training a Red or Orange dog, which involves suppressing the animal's overexuberance, in training a Green dog, you want to encourage the full expression of the his personality, attitude, and drive.

We can do this most readily by using treats or food rewards. If one of the few times your dog receives a treat or food reward is when you are training him, then it makes sense that he will look forward to the next training session. This joyful anticipation makes training fun for both you and your dog.

## Blue Dogs

Blue dogs are incredibly shy or intimidated, and most of the time their fear stems from negative experiences in their past. With the Blue dog, keep in mind that you are dealing with the *opposite* personality of the Red dog, so the training approach must be opposite as well.

It is also important for you to remember that, just as with Red, Orange, and Green dogs, there are various degrees of Blue. A dog that is all Blue is a complete introvert. When you are dealing with this type of dog, you *must* be patient

**This dog's fearful skittishness suggests an Extremely Blue dog. At this early point in training, he should receive a very gentle approach and lots of love.**

## PORTRAIT OF A BLUE DOG

For obvious reasons, Blue dogs are uncommon in the entertainment industry, and it is next to impossible to think of Blue dogs I have trained for movies, TV shows, or commercials. But there is one dog I worked with just recently that is an excellent example of an Extremely Blue dog. This dog actually belongs to my accountant, and a few years back my accountant asked me to come over and take a look at his dog. When I first saw Root Beer, I could see that he was incredibly fearful and comfortable only in certain areas of the house. What was amazing, though, was to see the dog's personality change once he got outside. When Root Beer was in the front yard, he was not nearly as timid as he was in certain areas in the house.

We worked on trying to make Root Beer more comfortable throughout the house. We also focused on why he was so much more comfortable outside the house. We started bringing him a little closer to the house each day. Root Beer continues to improve and is moving toward becoming a Green dog.

and understanding at all times. This is a point I cannot overemphasize.

Eliciting a Blue dog's interest in you will be even more challenging than doing so with a Green dog, but it is imperative that you capture the Blue's attention and retain it. As with the Green dog, you must work to coax out the Blue dog's personality and drive. You can best accomplish this goal with treats and food rewards. Believe me, training will be a more enjoyable journey for the both of you with a few tasty tidbits. Word to the wise: dogs look to us for trust, and in the beginning of training, a Blue dog needs that trust the most.

It is worth mentioning that perhaps because Yellow, Green, and Blue dogs are not known for being disruptive, many owners of animals with these personalities do not see

# PERSONALITY ADJUSTMENT/MERGING

Here's the great part: as you train your dog, his personality will begin to change as he starts to learn and as things get better.

- If your dog is Blue, he probably will not stay a Blue dog forever. Later, as he learns and becomes trained and gains more confidence, he will likely become a Green or Yellow dog.
- If your dog is Green, he will most likely become a Yellow dog.
- If your dog is Red, he will most likely become an Orange or Yellow dog.
- If your dog is Orange, he will most likely become a Yellow dog.
- If your dog is Yellow . . . lucky you!

As we continue to train our dogs, our goal is to get their personalities to shift closer to the center of our spectrum.

an immediate need for training. Not doing so, however, is a real mistake. I want to emphasize that training will *always* be beneficial to the dog as well as to you and your relationship with him.

Now that you understand the huge difference in training dogs with various personalities, can you imagine trying to train a Blue dog with the control that you use with a Red dog? The results could actually be devastating! Meanwhile, if you used the same type of motivation and attitude on a Red dog that you would use on a Blue, that dog would go bonkers! This mismatched training happens on a daily basis and on a massive scale. The result is thousands of dogs ending up in animal shelters and humane societies every year because the owners didn't take into account the personality of the dog they were working with.

OPPOSITE: When your dog is closer to the center of the color spectrum, he is neither fearful nor overwhelmed—he is at ease with you.

# Red Dogs

O f all the personalities, the ones many of you will find yourselves training in the beginning will probably be Red dogs. This high-strung and high-spirited dog should have a red light over his head, flashing the words *I'm out of control*—although not all Red dogs are exactly the same, they will have these qualities in common.

Like any of the colors, Red dogs come in all sizes and breeds. You may own a Fox Terrier, which is a very small dog, or you may own a large Rottweiler, and they both can be Red.

Remember, since these dogs have a turbo drive and upbeat personality, you're going to want to take the *opposite* tack in training them. You're going to do things that involve a lot of control because your dog is probably not going to want to sit still. Be the anchor, solid and secure; you

If you have friends who own a little Red dog, have you ever noticed what happens when you go to their house?

- As you knock on the door, you hear the little dog barking.
- Your friends will open the door, and the dog will continue to bark.
- As you walk in, the dog will probably bark and jump up on you for a few minutes, and then the whole thing is over (most of the time).
- When one of the guests starts talking to the little dog in a high-pitched voice, it increases the little dog's energy and excitement level, which makes the little dog start barking once more.

This is classic Red dog behavior.

must always remain in control. Use tactile rewards (petting and stroking) and a soft voice to calm your dog, but be very direct—just because you're not yelling does not mean you're not the boss.

The early training and care with this type of dog is going to require a lot of patience. The one serious mistake that I have seen many Red owners make in the beginning is displaying a great deal of negativity toward the dog and for the dog. They fall into this trap without realizing it. They constantly yank on the leash, raise their voices, or even get rough in handling the dog. This is the wrong way to start because it creates a negative introduction to training.

## TREATS

Most dogs naturally like treats or different types of food rewards. I think you'll find that your Red dog will not only like the treat but also get very excited when you bring it out or even show it to him—not the result you're looking for. Just by watching and learning how he responds to the treats, you can tell that this technique will only make him more difficult to control. Instead, focus on those tactile rewards. You have probably found a spot where your dog likes to be petted—make sure you remember where it is. Petting and stroking not only rewards the dog for doing a behavior correctly but also, in most cases, has a tendency to calm the dog down.

## YOUR ATTITUDE AND PERSONALITY

The way you act around your Red dog during a training session can absolutely work against you. If you're beginning a training session and your dog is on a leash and jumping around, what happens if you are jumping around as well? In most cases it will either keep the dog at the same excitement level or elevate it. Again, we want to calm the dog down. Act in a way that shows you are in control. By moving a little slower than normal or even staying in one place during most of the training session, you will serve as the much-needed anchor, steadying that wildly rocking furry boat.

This Red dog clearly responds well to being rewarded with petting and stroking—no need for a food reward.

## YOUR VOICE

It is *so* important to modulate your voice around Red dogs. Doing things such as talking in a high-pitched voice during a training session and having that high-pitched type of attitude can really make training difficult for you and your dog. Try doing things in the training session to calm and relax your Red dog. It's not volume that commands control; your dog will be paying much closer attention to your tone and your body language.

## TRIGGERS AND DESENSITIZATION

One of the defining characteristics of Red dogs is that so many things stimulate and excite them—in the extreme; it often seems that the slightest provocation makes them lose their cool. So many owners of Red dogs become frustrated with their dogs in these early stages of training because without even knowing it, they are reinforcing their animals' out-of-control behavior. Just by using treats, increasing their excitement levels, and raising their voices, they are making the process a whole lot harder.

As discussed in chapter 1, avoid using treats or anything that will make your dog more overexcited and easily distracted. I would not recommend clicker training for this dog (see page 89). You also need to identify your dog's specific triggers and deal with them immediately. For instance, small animals, such as squirrels, may make your Red dog go bonkers; so, too, may a knock at the front door. Keep in mind that the warmer the dog, the smaller the trigger needed to excite him. What stirs up a Red dog may not even appear on the radar of a cooler-colored dog, such as a Yellow or a Green.

When you identify your dog's triggers, you need to begin desensitizing him to them. *Desensitization* means gradually exposing your dog to the various distractions and getting him to a place where he is no longer distracted by them during training sessions. What once triggered a frenzy will soon become old hat. and as your dog gets more and more comfortable, he will begin to calm down.

# SHADES OF RED

The great part about training Red dogs is that no matter where they fall on the Red end of the spectrum, they are happy, excited, energetic, and eager to please. You want to take advantage of that state and maintain it during your training sessions. As you forge ahead, you will see that your dog will learn some behaviors more quickly than others, so remain patient and be sensitive to just how Red he is. Below are some variations you might notice.

## EXTREMELY RED DOG

Periodically, you will hear me say "Extremely Red" when I am talking about certain dogs. Reining these dogs in may appear nearly impossible at first; they can be the most unruly, the most berserk, and the most neurotic dogs around, with a tendency to bounce off the training walls, if you let them. Think of this type of dog as being "on fire." But don't get discouraged. With an Extremely Red dog, most of the problems you'll encounter will be at the very beginning of training. Persistence and patience, which are vital to success, can pay off, and you'll eventually be able to turn this bright Red dog down a notch or two, at the very least.

## RED DOG

The majority of Red dogs will fit under this heading. You can usually get a handle on these high-strung canines, but it's never easy. However, with many of these dogs, you will find that once they do begin to relax, they have the ability to learn very quickly—great! Encourage your dog to learn the basic commands taught in the following chapters, and you might see his bold Red flame flicker down to Orange in no time at all.

## RED/ORANGE DOG

Maybe this dog naturally has a tendency to excite easily, but he's more controllable than the typical Red dog. A Red/Orange dog will most likely be even easier to work with initially, since he's even closer to that desirable mellow Yellow.

The essential thing early on is to identify your dog's degree of Redness and proceed accordingly. As your dog becomes trained, settles down, and begins to understand what you want, he will start to change color. Just think about bringing the color of your dog toward the center of our spectrum, getting him to "cool down."

# TRAINING TIPS FOR YOUR RED DOG

Remember that early on you are going to want to do things that involve using more control than you would with any of the other color dogs. A great example is spending a little more time closer to your dog when he is being trained to sit. The reason for this is that the Red dog is apt to be a lot more out of control and is likely to get up. Your goal should be to start stepping back and training the stay once the Red dog is consistent with just sitting.

Once your Red dog begins to understand the sit and stay and develops control, he will learn amazingly fast.

Believe it or not, there are some professional animal trainers that absolutely love training Red dogs because of their high drive. Red dogs with a high prey drive combined with the Extremely Red attitude often make great bomb dogs, drug dogs, and patrol dogs. They can also make great agility dogs!

In most cases, once a Red dog of any degree is trained to simply sit and stay, he will gain some control and begin to change colors: Extremely Red to Red, and Red to Orange. To summarize, understand that Red dogs are very smart. Once they begin to learn and start having fun, you will be amazed at their true potential and what they are capable of.

**OPPOSITE:** Training a high-octane Red dog can be not only challenging but also a great deal of fun!

# Orange Dogs

G iven the nature of most young and untrained dogs, it is easy to see how they are usually Red or Orange. The Orange dog is fairly high-strung and energetic. From a professional animal trainer's perspective, it is the dog that most people would like to begin with because Orange dogs not only have an incredible amount of energy but also show a willingness to please.

As you know, there's no size requirement for an energetic dog, so your Orange dog can be anything from a hot-wired Cairn Terrier to a bouncy Bearded Collie.

Although they share several traits with the Red dog, Orange dogs do not come close to that level of intensity. With an Orange dog that leans toward Yellow, you are going to have an easier time training, as his demeanor will be tempered by the mellow characteristics

of the Yellow. However, an Orange dog that leans toward Red will be harder to corral and will require a bit more patience.

You want to adopt an attitude opposite that of your dog's when you begin training; in other words, the more hyperactive he is, the calmer you will need to be. Remember to stay in control and avoid anything that might increase his agitation (such as introducing food rewards). When your Orange dog demonstrates a behavior correctly, petting and stroking his favorite spot should be all the reward that he needs to receive.

However, an Orange dog that leans toward Yellow in the beginning will be a little different. This is a dog that you may be able to introduce treats to without the dog's becoming out of control. Of course, this will make training a great deal easier because you will have more rewards to offer him.

Your Orange dog will certainly appreciate some post-training affection, regardless of his demeanor.

## PREY DRIVE IN THE MOVIES

Orange and Red dogs usually have some prey drive. That was fortunate for a Jack Russell Terrier named Sunshine and me when the director of the 2006 movie *A Good Year* needed a feisty terrier for a part.

Many Jack Russell Terriers start off as Red or Orange dogs. I got Sunshine as a puppy, and she was Orange/Yellow, which made her very easy to train. For the movie, which was filmed in southern France, I trained Sunshine to grab Russell Crowe's pant leg. That kind of behavior is easiest to train with an Orange or Red dog; a Green or Blue dog just will not want to be that outgoing.

Initially, you may find Orange dogs to be outgoing and possibly a little obnoxious. Be patient. Training should not be a negative experience for your dog. By yelling or over-correcting with the use of a chain collar, you can very easily fall into that trap. You will to want to prepare yourself for a dog with a lot of energy, even before you bring him out for his first session.

The word I use often in training Orange dogs is *control.* Orange dogs do not like to laze about and do nothing; you will need to be extra vigilant that your dog is where he needs to be, when he needs to be there. It is essential that you prepare for this by paying attention to the following four points.

### TREATS

It's no surprise that most dogs are motivated by food and will rally for a treat. If you find that your Orange dog leans toward Yellow or will work for a tasty morsel or two, my suggestion would be to offer him a biscuit style of treat or give him something dry. Dry liver treats work very well, too. The last thing you want to do with a dog that may get a little rambunctious over a treat is to use particularly savory

Act calm and confident to counteract your Orange dog's tendencies toward distraction.

foods, such as real meat or cheese: you want him motivated, not bonkers. Always make certain that you are aware of the dog's response to the treats that you introduce.

If your dog leans toward Red or you decide to stay away from treats in the initial training, I highly recommend using tactile rewards.

## YOUR ATTITUDE AND PERSONALITY

Your own behavior around your Orange dog during a training session can make your naturally excitable pooch Redder. You'll find that your dog will stay stoked or turn up the heat if you begin to get excited, too. The dog will then become even less controllable. Keep in mind that we are trying to calm the dog down; this is why I recommend that you act cool and collected. Move slower than usual, and set yourself in one place for most of your dog's early training sessions—this will help your Orange dog settle down. I would not recommend clicker training with this warm-color dog (see page 89).

The terrific news is that Orange dogs in general are happy-go-lucky, energetic, and naturally focused on you. An Orange dog should respond to your lead more readily than will his Red counterparts. If you capitalize on these innate traits of Orange dogs, you can bank on having fun with them in training. Some of the best dogs in the film and television industries started off as Orange dogs, with great attitudes and personalities.

## YOUR VOICE

The way you talk to an Orange dog can either increase the excitement level or calm the dog down. Talking in a high-pitched voice to your Orange Dog during a training session and being very animated can make training your dog more difficult. Go back to the scenario in which you act like an anchor, and do things in the training session to calm and relax your dog. You do not need to be loud with your dog; just make sure that your voice commands control.

**When a dog is as excited as this Golden Retriever, use a soothing voice.**

## TRAINING TIPS FOR YOUR ORANGE DOG

Try to identify early on whether you are able to use treats with your Orange dog without causing him to lose control. If your dog becomes too excited, just use tactile rewards. Your main goal should be to get him to the point where he will accept treats and stay in control.

In most cases, once your Orange dog is trained to sit and stay and gain some control, he will begin to move toward being a Yellow dog.

Most professional animal trainers prefer working with Orange dogs from the beginning because of their intelligence and attitude of wanting to please. Just be very patient with these dogs.

## TRIGGERS AND DESENSITIZATION

If you look at the spectrum, the goal is to get your Orange dog to move in the Yellow direction. Remember, you always want the color of your dog to move toward the center of our spectrum and begin to "cool down." With the right training, this can happen pretty quickly, too!

To accomplish this, you should first identify any triggers that might excite your Orange dog. Many of the elements that stir up a Red dog will do so with an Orange one as well, although often to a lesser extent (that is, he will not go as crazy!). These triggers can include bicycles, skateboards, kids playing, and other animals.

Once you determine the triggers, you need to start desensitizing your dog to them. *Desensitization* means exposing your dog to these distractions gradually and getting him to a point at which they no longer distract him. As your dog gets more and more comfortable around those triggers, he will begin to calm down. For more training tips to use with Orange dogs, see the box above.

**OPPOSITE:** Yellow TV star Bear began professional life as an Orange dog. Trainers like working with Orange dogs, which have a Red's energy but take instruction better.

# Yellow Dogs

**Y**ellow dogs, the "middle-of-the-road" dogs, are often the easiest to train from the beginning. There are some distinguishing behavioral characteristics of the Yellow dog; the first one that always comes to mind is the dog's laid-back personality.

The reason Yellow dogs are positioned in the center of the spectrum is that they lack the extreme characteristics of Blue and Red dogs. They are neither excessively shy nor hyperactive. Because this type of dog is almost always easier to train, this chapter is fairly short.

However, don't make the mistake of thinking of Yellow dogs as plain and boring. You'll find that their personalities can change—once a relationship has been established with their owners, their attitude and personality will begin to develop and express

## A DOG AND HIS ORPHAN ANNIE

About ten years ago, I built a team of dogs for a company that supplies animals for movies, TV shows, and commercials. Chester was one of the first dogs that I adopted. Chester was for sure a mellow Yellow dog. As I remember, he was pretty much always that way, too. He ended up being one of the best working dogs in the industry, thanks to his naturally lovable and sweet Yellow personality. He landed his biggest role in 1999, playing Sandy in the TV movie *Annie*, starring Kathy Bates.

itself more fully. There are things you can do to raise the dog's energy level if you want to. You can also take action to calm the dog down if needed. In essence, Yellow dogs will look to you for guidance and will be motivated by the things you do.

### TREATS

Most Yellow dogs like a variety of rewards, so you should try different things. Training will become more interesting to your dog as you offer a greater array of incentives. You might find that some types of treats will elevate your dog's personality and others will keep him calmer—these are things you especially want to be aware of, so you can introduce those treats at the most opportune times.

### YOUR ATTITUDE, PERSONALITY, AND VOICE

Through your own actions, you have the ability to make training interesting for your Yellow dog. By changing things up and staying unpredictable, you will keep training fun for him and for you.

You are going to find that when you begin giving cues to your dog, the tone of your voice really will not change much at all. I have found that one of the luxuries in training Yellow dogs is that almost all of the cues I give them can

This Yellow dog looks relaxed and happy. Many times, Yellow dogs play off of your attitude and personality—if you're excited about training, so are they.

be done in my normal tone of voice. People often say to me, in surprise, "You are so soft-spoken when you are training your dog!"

## TRIGGERS AND DESENSITIZATION

Yellow dogs usually don't have as many triggers as other color dogs do, but they can be distracted by certain things. One of the ways to ensure that your dog remains Yellow is to expose him to as many distractions as possible early on. You want him to be aware of people, animals, objects, and other aspects of his environment, such as the variety of sights, smells, and sounds.

If for some reason you see the dog develop a minor fear, address it immediately through desensitization. That means exposing him to the object *gradually*. For instance, if your dog is afraid of skateboards, don't position him right next to a person with skateboard; instead, find the distance at which he is comfortable. If that is 50 yards away, then that

Yellow dogs respond well to a lot of variety in their training sessions, so be sure to mix it up!

# TRAINING TIPS FOR YOUR YELLOW DOG

If you think your Yellow dog is rambunctious and needs more control in training, you will want to use more of the techniques you would use with an Orange or Red dog.

If the dog would benefit from greater energy and motivation, you will use more training techniques like those most appropriate for a Green or Blue dog. These techniques will help you bring out the underlying personality of your Yellow dog.

*Variety* is another beneficial influence for a Yellow dog. Dogs like variation, and Yellow dogs tend to like it most. Variation involves constantly mixing it up and keeping your dog guessing. For instance, you can vary the types of rewards you offer. You might use soft liver treats some of the time and cheese at other times; then you might use a toy as a reward and then a tactile reward. All of this variety keeps it fun and interesting. Remember that change is reinforcing to an animal.

is your starting point. Each day, you will move the dog a little bit closer to the skateboarder. Before you know it, he will be doing fine at a distance of 10 feet.

## CHANGEABLE TECHNIQUES

The most appropriate training techniques are going to vary depending on your Yellow dog. At times, when you want to get more motivation and attitude out of your dog, you will find yourself using techniques geared toward training a Green dog or a Blue dog. At other times, when you are looking for control and a little more command of your dog, you will find yourself using techniques geared toward training an Orange dog or a Red dog.

In summary, to understand the training of the Yellow dog, it helps to understand the extreme behavioral characteristics of the Blue and Red dogs. These two color groups have totally different personalities, and because of that, the training is as different as night and day. To aid in training your Yellow dog, I recommend reading the chapters on the other colors.

# Green Dogs

G reen dogs can come in any size, shape, and color, but I must say that the majority I have seen have been small dogs. It's really no surprise when you think of small breeds such as Chihuahuas, Pekingese, Yorkshire Terriers, and Maltese. These breeds tend to walk through life a little fearfully, probably because of their size. (They know they can be stepped on, because they have been!) This is not to say that you will not discover a few Yellow or Orange pups in a litter of Chihuahuas. However, many of the smaller breeds have an inclination toward shyness or apprehension, especially around new people.

Whatever the reason for these traits, these dogs have the same intelligence and the same learning potential as Yellow, Orange, and Red dogs do. Once you learn how to reduce the level of his shyness or fear, you'll be amazed at some of the things your Green dog can learn.

Apprehensive Green dogs, such as this one, can go either Blue or Yellow in training. It's up to you to make sure he gets warmer, not cooler, in color.

There is a good possibility that your dog acts the way he does because of incidents from his past; he may not have been properly trained or cared for, or he may have been abused or frightened.

With the Green dog, as with the Orange dog, remember that we are now between an extreme personality and an ideal personality. Therefore, you must train accordingly. When you train a dog with an extreme personality, you will have to be much more patient. For example, with a Blue dog that is very fearful of many things, you will need to spend a lot of time simply building the trust before the training even begins. A Green dog will not have that level of fear and will not require as much time.

Consider also the various degrees of Green. A dog that leans toward Blue will be even more timorous or withdrawn. That level of Green might take a little more time and patience. A dog that is less reserved might lean toward

Yellow. If you are training a Green dog that leans toward Yellow, you will have an easier time with him; he will be mellower and more receptive to your instruction.

When training Green dogs, you must find a way to keep them motivated by and interested in you. Your first goal with a Green dog is to help him with his fears and shyness. Your second goal is to bring out the Green dog's hidden personality, attitude, and drive. Treats and food rewards should accomplish this nicely.

The traits you'll see in Green dogs are not nearly as extreme as those of Blue dogs, but there are some similarities. When you're initially training a Green dog, you need to remember that this dog can have a negative attitude toward wanting to learn anything; often this is the direct result of previous attempts at training. If the dog has not had fun being trained in the past, it will be entirely up to you to change his outlook.

## MAKING A GREEN DOG COMFORTABLE

My dog Foster, who is featured in this book, is a Green dog. One of the drawbacks of working with a Green dog is that there are some situations and objects that might initially scare or worry him. But once you have built the trust and relationship with a dog such as Foster, if he has an issue, within a few minutes he understands that everything is OK, and he is ready to work.

When I am working with a Green dog, I always take time to bring him to the set to allow him to get comfortable with the environment. In Foster's case, I allow him to meet the actors and crew ahead of time. If I fail to take this precaution, he might be a little apprehensive and come across as a bit afraid on camera.

Although sometimes their fears obscure the fact, one of the great aspects of Green dogs is that many of them are extremely smart. Foster certainly is!

## TREATS

Giving a Green dog a treat will actually excite him and increase his energy level. Just watch your dog and note how he responds to different treats; the ones he goes crazy over are the ones that I'd recommend using in the training session.

## USE OF THE CLICKER

Although I would not necessarily recommend clicker training with the warmer-colored dogs, with a Green or Blue dog it can be a great idea. I think you will find that clicker training will increase the motivation and desire to learn of these dogs.

The idea behind the clicker is to pair it with the treat each time you reward the dog. Each time the dog does something you like, press the clicker once and immediately give the dog a treat.

As your dog becomes a little more advanced, you can begin to vary the times you feed him after you click. One

Using a clicker with a Green dog can be a big help in motivation as well as enjoyment.

example is you might click once (which tells the dog the action he took was correct) and then immediately give him another cue to do something else. The next time you might click (which tells the dog the action he took was correct) and then immediately give him a treat. This variation is an important factor in successful clicker training. The best animal trainers understand that the clicker should mean "You responded with the correct behavior," not "I have a treat for you."

## YOUR ATTITUDE AND PERSONALITY

The way you act around your Green dog during a training session can either calm your dog or elevate his excitement level. If you have your dog on a leash and have some treats in your hand and start moving around, what do you think your dog will be doing? He'll probably be watching you. What do you want him to be watching and paying attention to in the session? You! If you become more animated and start moving about, your dog will become more excited as well, bringing you both closer to training success.

## YOUR VOICE

Talking in a high-pitched voice or with some excitement in your voice can really increase your Green dog's interest level in a training session. This is another way to make training a fun and positive experience that the animal will look forward to.

## TRIGGERS AND DESENSITIZATION

Remember that the Green Dog will most likely not remain an Extremely Green Dog. As your dog gets over some issues, develops confidence, and becomes more secure within himself, his color will change and begin to "warm up." If the training is successful, your Green dog should become Yellow. Of all the dog color types, I think that individual personalities can vary the most among Green dogs. My suggestion is to take some time and really get to know your dog to learn what situations and objects he may fear.

## TRAINING TIPS FOR YOUR GREEN DOG

Avoid using chain collars on fearful Green dogs, and be aware of your corrections. Sometimes you don't need to raise your voice, even if you are saying the word *no*.

In most cases, once a Green dog is trained to sit and stay, he will begin to become more Yellow. Remember that Yellow dogs are mellow and laid-back, and they can show a lot of independence. Once the Green dogs learn to sit and stay, you can begin to create a little distance between you and the dog, and he will start to lose the codependency many Green dogs possess.

Green dogs are really hidden jewels. They have a lot of potential but often do not show it right away. Once training becomes fun for them, they have the ability to learn just as much as any Yellow, Orange, or Red dog can.

If you can successfully identify some of your Green dog's fear triggers early on, it is amazing how much your dog's sense of confidence can improve. After you identify what things your dog fears, you will want to take time to desensitize him to these triggers. As you begin to expose your dog to these factors, you can get him to a place where the distractions are no longer distractions: as your dog becomes more and more comfortable around them, he will begin to calm down.

**OPPOSITE: You may need to be creative in order to focus your Green dog's attention where it is needed most—on you.**

# Blue Dogs

The personalities of Blue dogs and Red dogs are complete opposites. Think of the most bashful, cringing, slinking dog you know. Chances are he's a Blue. This could just be the way he was born, but these traits have more likely been reinforced by past events. Regardless of why your Blue dog is so submissive, take comfort in knowing that he possesses the same intelligence and potential to learn as do dogs from every other color of the "trainbow."

So just how Blue is he? Your dog may be intensely nervous and fearful, which would put him on the far end of the spectrum as an Extremely Blue dog. If your dog is only shy in specific situations, his personality type may be a little closer to that of the Green dog. Regardless of how Blue your dog is initially, it is unlikely that his individual shade will remain the

same throughout training. As your dog gets over some issues, develops confidence, and becomes more secure, his color will begin to warm up.

You should expect a Blue dog to resist the initial steps in training for some good reasons—he may be afraid or convinced training will be about as enjoyable as eating a bowl of rocks. You *can* break through that wall of resistance. By building trust and emphasizing those things your dog likes, you will be astonished by what your Blue dog can learn. How do we deal with all this negativity? Whereas Red dogs must be trained with lots of control, Blue dogs are just the opposite. They need to be worked up—motivated, inspired, energized—depending on the degree of Blue traits they exhibit.

It is imperative in training a Blue dog that you find a way to get the dog interested in you. As is the case for the Green dog, we want to bring out the Blue dog's personality, attitude, and drive. This is done *with* treats or food rewards. If one of the few times your dog gets treats or food rewards is when you are training him, it stands to reason that the animal will look forward to the training session. If that happens, training becomes fun for both you and your dog. All dogs look to us for trust, but in the beginning of training, a Blue dog needs it most.

## A CLASSIC BLUE

If you have friends who own a Blue dog and you visit their house, in many cases you will notice the following chain of events:

- As you knock on the door, the dog runs into another room and hides.
- You enter the house, and the dog remains hidden.
- After a few minutes, the dog slowly comes out from where he was. (Extremely Blue dogs may not come out at all while you're there.)
- You approach and try to pet the dog, and he runs away.

This is classic Blue dog behavior.

When starting to train a Blue dog, more of your patience and encouragement may be required than with dogs of other colors.

This increased motivation will make the Blue dog look forward to interacting with you and taking part in training sessions. There are special methods you can use to encourage this sense of anticipation in Blue dogs, but sometimes just the way you handle them, talk to them, guide them, and reward them will help. Remember that your Blue dog's motivation comes directly from you. For example, if you are training a small or medium-size Blue dog, you want to try to get down to the dog's level or raise the dog to yours using an elevated surface. Take the time to relate to your dog, perhaps by petting him in a favorite place or just keeping him near you. This might not mean as much to other color dogs, but it means the world to a Blue.

There are times when an owner may move a little too cautiously around a Blue dog, transmitting uncertainty to him. Try to keep your movements more natural. This type of body language will motivate your dog and make him look forward to you and the training session.

## TREATS

Most dogs like treats or different types of food rewards. You'll find that your Blue dog will not only like the treat but also get excited and show an increased level of energy. Watch your dog and learn how he responds to different treats to discover which ones he likes best. For training sessions, I recommend using the treats he goes crazy over. This will serve to increase the Blue dog's sense of anticipation and excitement to an optimal level.

## USE OF THE CLICKER

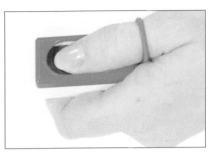

I would not necessarily recommend clicker training with every color type of dog, but I would recommend it for the Blue dog. Clicker training will increase the animal's motivation and desire to learn by improving his confidence. Pair the clicker with the treat each time you feed him; once the dog does something you like, click the clicker once and immediately give the dog his yummy reward.

Just as with the Green dog, as your Blue dog becomes more advanced, you can vary the times you feed him after you click. For example, you might click one time (which tells the dog he did something right) and then immediately give him another cue to do something else. The next time you might click (which tells the dog the thing he did was correct) and then immediately give him a treat. This variation is key in effective dog training. The best animal trainers understand that the clicker should mean "You did the behavior correctly," not "I have a treat for you."

## YOUR ATTITUDE AND PERSONALITY

The way you act around your Blue dog during a training session can either calm your dog or elevate his excitement level. For instance, if you have your dog on a leash and have some treats in your hand and start moving around, what do you think your dog's response will be? He will probably be watching your every move. If you become a little more animated and start moving around a little more, your dog's level of excitement and curiosity will rise. You have the ability to increase your dog's energy and attitude through your movements and actions.

# TRAINING TIPS FOR YOUR BLUE DOG

Avoid using chain collars on Blue dogs, and be aware of your corrections. Never raise your voice with a dog of this color, even when you are saying the word *no*.

Blue dogs don't always show their cards, so to speak. As you get to know him, develop a relationship, and become his friend, a Blue dog sometimes begins acting like an entirely different dog. Shower your dog with affection, give him your time and attention, and keep him close to you—he may just blossom.

## YOUR VOICE

If you talk in a high-pitched voice or with some excitement in your voice, you can increase your Blue dog's excitement level in a training session. This is just another way of making training a fun and positive thing the animal will look forward to.

## TRIGGERS AND DESENSITIZATION

The Blue dog is the dog that will need by far the most patience as you watch for improvements in his behavior. That's because this animal will have an enormous amount of fear and anxiety. Therefore, even before you begin training, you must deal with the fear issues and get the animal as comfortable as possible. The first step is to get to know your dog, understand him, and develop a trusting relationship with him. This is true for all dogs, but it is critical for Blue and Extremely Blue dogs. This can take considerable time to accomplish.

Once you have trust, you can identify your dog's fear triggers and help him deal with them. Once you have identified some of your dog's triggers, *slowly and patiently* begin to desensitize him to them. This means you are going to start exposing your dog to these distractions on a limited basis to the point at which he is no longer affected. As your dog becomes more comfortable around those distractions, he will begin to loosen up. With this process, you will instill courage and confidence in your Blue dog—and that will make him easier to train.

# Training Tools

I am sure that all of you who are reading this book have different jobs. There are many things that allow you to do your job effectively and efficiently, but most of all you require the correct tools. You don't necessarily need a lot of them, but you do have to have the right ones. In dog training, the same rule applies.

Depending on the color of dog you are working with, the tools can vary, but one tool is essential for all dogs: the leash. No matter what color your dog may be, you must always have a leash on him during training. This gives you control over your dog, including the ability to keep him exactly where you want him.

If your dog is not on a leash, you will find yourself calling him again and again, trying to get his attention. You will end up frustrated and impatient with him—not a good frame of mind for training.

## LEASHES

Dog leashes come in almost every size and color imaginable. When you are deciding which leash to purchase, you must take into account the personality (color) and size of your particular dog.

Let's say that you have two small dogs. One of them is a Red Parson Russell Terrier, and the other is a small mutt that happens to be Blue. You can use the same length of leash with these dogs—4 to 6 feet—and because they are of a similar size, you can use the same thickness—a quarter to a half inch.

The difference will be in the type of leash and what it's made of. With the Red Parson Russell Terrier—a dog that is going to pull—you will want to use a leather leash because it will be a lot easier on your hands.

With the small Blue dog, however, you may not need to use anything as expensive as a leather leash because he is less likely to pull. So a lighter and less costly nylon leash will do just fine.

You can use this same scenario for larger dogs. The only aspect that really will change is the thickness of the leash.

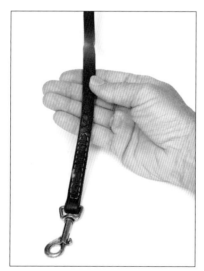

Get a thin leather leash, easy on the hands, for a small Red or Orange dog.

Use a wider, stronger leather leash for a medium or large Red or Orange dog.

With a larger Red dog, you might be using a 6-foot leather leash that is a half to 1 inch wide. With a large Blue dog, you might use a 6-foot nylon leash, which is lighter for your dog, because, again, he probably won't be pulling as much.

## COLLARS

If you're training a Blue or Green dog, you will simply use the collar that the dog normally wears every day. A Yellow dog may also do best with his regular collar, unless he leans toward Orange. Make sure that the collar is tight enough so that it does not slip over your dog's head during the training session, yet not too tight. A useful guideline is that if you can fit three fingers between the dog's collar and the dog's neck, the fit is ideal (see page 70).

### The Chain Collar

I recommend using a chain collar when training Red, Orange, and Orange-leaning Yellow dogs, but you will *not* want to use a chain collar with Green dogs and Blue dogs. The chain collar—or choke chain, as many people call it—is a great tool in training when it is used the right way. Given how effective a tool the chain collar can be, I am amazed that so many people have issues with its use.

**When used properly, a chain collar can be an effective training tool.**

Hundreds of people who previously had a negative reaction to the use of chain collars have implemented my technique. They seemingly just needed some clarification to understand how to use chain collars correctly. There are many misconceptions about these collars. Some people will not use this tool because it is commonly called a *choke* chain. I just read a claim that the chain collar "cuts off air to your dog for a brief instant."

If you are abusive to your dog and hold him off the ground, yes, a chain collar will cut off his air supply. It's important to understand, though, that an inhumane person who would hold the dog off the ground would find a way to abuse his dog with or without a chain collar.

In the wrong situation with the wrong dog, there is no question that a chain collar can be the wrong tool. In fact, I am sure that thousands of dogs have ended up in animal shelters and humane societies over the years just because the wrong person *was* using a chain collar on the wrong dog. That is exactly why I have separated my training based on colors, or personalities.

It is usually the person at the end of the leash attached to the chain collar who is to blame, not the tool in and of

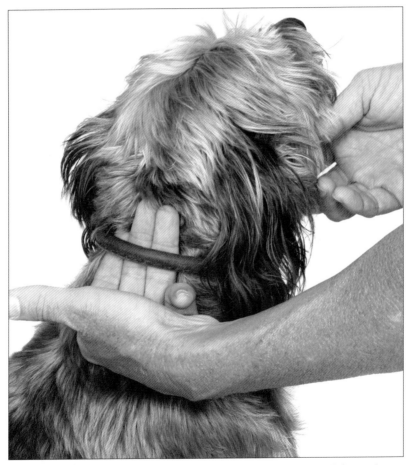

To check the fit of your dog's collar, try to slip three fingers beneath it, as shown here. This is a perfect fit.

itself. In my opinion, there are three reasons why a dog might have had some sort of aversive reaction to or fear of the chain collar in the past:

- The person handling the dog was an abusive person. It did not matter whether the person used a chain collar; he would have found some way or another to abuse the animal.
- The person training the dog was using a chain collar on a Blue or Green dog, which is typically the wrong personality type for the use of this tool.
- And the most common reason: the person handling the dog was never taught how to properly use a chain collar or how to put one on the animal. Without the proper understanding, the owner either corrects the dog too hard or does not correct the dog enough.

By the way, if you're looking for the people who have never learned how to correct their dogs hard enough, it's fairly easy to do. These would be the ones with the *pinch collars* on their dogs.

## The Pinch Collar

If you have never seen one of these before, notice there are many prongs that compress the neck as the collar is pulled (note also that these collars are illegal in the United Kingdom). I have never used a pinch collar myself, and I have seen this tool used on numerous occasions when it could have been avoided.

The prongs of the pinch collar "pinch" the dog's neck when tightened.

Here are a few reasons why owners might resort to the use of a pinch collar:

- The owner may not have ever learned how to correctly put a chain collar on the dog and so does not have the control he desires.

- The owner may never have learned how to use a chain collar properly. As a result, he may not have corrected the dog hard enough because he thought that the correction was abusive or painful for the dog. Once this has occurred, the dog will not respect the chain collar.
- The owner may never have used a chain collar at all in the early stages of training.

Any problem with the chain collar is most likely the result of the owner's not being educated in the first place. If you own a very large, out-of-control dog and don't know how to use a chain collar effectively, chances are you will either continue having an out-of-control dog or end up using a pinch collar. Which do you think can be more painful to your dog? Take a look at the photo at the bottom of the page and make the decision for yourself.

I have learned over the years that there are no absolutes, and although I have never ever used a pinch collar and never worked with any dog trainer who did, there might be rare cases in which the owner has no other option. An example would be a 90-pound woman with a 140-pound dog that is out of control. In that scenario, the owner may not have any choice in the matter. If she wants

Only under extreme circumstances (such as having an out-of-control dog that greatly outweighs you) should you pick a pinch collar (left) over a chain collar (right).

to maintain control of her large dog, she has to utilize the pinch collar.

As I discussed earlier, even the chain collar is not appropriate for every dog. If you have a Yellow dog, you really need to look at that dog and determine whether you need to use a chain collar on him. What you will probably find is that with the majority of Yellow dogs, you can do fine without one.

## ELEVATED AREA

Train your dog on an elevated area. If you're working with a small dog, you could work on something such as a bed, a couch, or a chair. If you are dealing with a larger dog, you could work on something slightly elevated, such as a low porch. Putting the animal in a defined elevated area that serves as a designated training area facilitates control of the dog. The problem with training on flat ground is that, because there is no designated training area, your dog can wander. As you will learn, the elevated area makes the training of the stay behavior easier for you and your dog, because

Working with your dog on an elevated area makes training easier for him and on your back.

## PUTTING ON THE CHAIN COLLAR

There is a right way and a wrong way to put on a chain collar. When it is put on properly, you will see that it functions properly, but if it is put on the wrong way, you will have difficulty right from the start.

On this page, you can see the *right* way to put on the chain collar. On the opposite page, you can see the *wrong* way. In both sets of photos, the dog is facing away from us and is on the left side. Look at where the leash connects to the chain collar on this page. Now follow the chain as it goes through the ring. Is the chain going around the outside edge of the ring or on the dog's side of the ring? You can see that it is going around the *outside*. Now take a look at the next page and see where the leash connects to the chain collar. If you follow where it connects to the chain and goes through that ring, is the chain going around the dog's side of the ring or the outside of the ring? You can see that the chain goes beneath the dog.

**The part of the chain the leash attaches to goes around the outside. Right!**

**Therefore, when the trainer pulls, all tension comes from the outside.**

Now examine the differences in how the force is applied. In the first set of images, if the owner pulls on the dog to correct him, you can see that the force comes from the outside edge of the ring. This is because the part of the collar the owner is pulling on goes around the *outside* edge of the ring, away from the dog. This makes correcting the dog a lot easier for the owner.

On this page, if the owner pulls on the dog to correct him, the force comes from *under* the dog's neck. This is because the part of the collar that the owner is pulling on comes from *under* the dog. This makes correcting the dog a lot more difficult for the owner, in that when the owner goes to correct the dog, he is actually lifting up on the animal. There are two major problems that can arise from this. The first is that correcting the dog will be much harder for the owner, since he now needs to lift up on the dog. The second is that since the dog is not corrected enough to have an impact, the chain collar becomes a useless tool and the dog learns that he can get away with something. This could lead to many other behavior problems.

The best way to understand this is by trying to put on the chain collar both the right way and the wrong way. Once you correct your dog a few times, you will see how much easier the right way is for the two of you.

The part of the chain the leash attaches to goes under the dog's neck. Wrong!

Therefore, when the trainer pulls, all the tension comes from under the dog.

when the dog ventures off the elevated area onto flat ground, it is clear to you and the dog that he is not "staying." Working on an elevated area can also make training easier on your back.

## REWARDS

One of the first things to understand about training animals is that they all need rewards or reinforcements. Sometimes it can be a good idea to put yourself in your dog's position. If you think of yourself and your workplace, you need to know that the work you do is appreciated. That is the reason you get raises (or do not get raises), and the same principle applies to animals. Depending on the color, or the personality, of the particular the dog you are training, the nature of the best reward will vary immensely.

In general, you will be using food rewards for Blue, Green, and some Yellow dogs. In some instances with Orange dogs, if your dog is not a Red-leaning dog, you might find that you can use treats. You will determine which type of reward to use in the first thirty days or so of training, while assessing your dog's personality, likes, and dislikes.

An especially savory morsel, like this bit of meat, should entice a disinterested Green or Blue dog.

I always recommend purchasing a little bag to wear on your belt to put the treats in. This works great because it frees up your hands during training. Once you do find the special treat that your dog adores, try to give him that treat only in training sessions or at other special times. This will make training something that your dog looks forward to. Remember that with Blue dogs in particular, we're really trying to get them interested in us and the training session. If there is something that the dog can look forward to in the training session that he never gets at any other time, it will make things that much easier.

In the training of Red and Extremely Red dogs and Red-leaning Orange dogs, you will *not* be using food. Since we know treats can intensify dogs' personalities, we must steer toward tactile rewards (petting) instead when working with a dog that needs to be soothed rather than agitated.

You will find that most Red dogs naturally want to please you and will feel validated simply by getting your approval, maybe combined with a nice rub. This approach is similar to that used for the training of marine mammals. In working with dolphins, sea lions, and orcas (killer whales), I have found that they like to receive different types of rewards; if I vary the rewards, training is more interesting and fun for them. Your dog might prefer one among a variety of things—a specific toy, for example. Once you identify that object, you can use it as a reward at the end of the session. Varying the routine so that your dog doesn't know what type of reward will be coming will ensure that his level of enthusiasm and attention will remain high and that training will be exciting and fun for both you and your dog.

# Training Techniques

Over the years, I have heard about many training ideas and techniques. Some have come and gone; others remain. Because all dogs have different personalities, certain aspects of certain techniques are going to work better for certain dogs than they do for others. The mistake lies in thinking that one technique will work on every dog.

If you look at all the training techniques out there, they cover a spectrum. People on one end tout their technique as involving "no correction," as being "only positive" or "non-aversive" training. People on the other end use techniques involving too much force and negativity and not enough fun. Then there are the trainers who say, "You need to be the alpha dog." That is fine if you are training or living with a pack of dogs, but most people have just one or two.

Before discussing some of these training techniques, I want to

There are a variety of reasons a dog may try to bite, but humans are frequently to blame.

offer a word of warning about the problem of aggression. Of all the dogs that I have rescued or encountered, only 2 percent or so have been aggressive, But it can happen. Most of the aggression I have seen developed from the way the animal had been cared for or trained. It seems that, more often than not, dogs become aggressive based on our responses to their actions.

Signs of aggression include, but are not limited to:

• Growling or barking at certain people
• Growling, snapping, or barking when petted
• Playing so roughly that it segues into aggression
• Being overly possessive of toys

If you see your dog exhibiting behaviors you think may be some form of aggression, immediately call a professional dog trainer who deals specifically with this problem.

## "NO CORRECTION" TRAINING

People who support this extreme approach believe that the animal should never receive a correction. After speaking with many of them, I have found that they simply do not understand what a correction is. Some of them also believe that you should never say the word *no* to your dog, because they define that as a "correction," something that is negative. Unfortunately, the people who use this type of training are living in a dream world. No successful animal trainer I have ever met in all my years of training has bought this method.

I am always amazed when I hear people talk about the "no correction" method of training. It shocks me because I think of animals as being so much like people, and I wonder what a child would be like if she grew up never knowing right from wrong because no one had ever corrected her unacceptable behavior. The child would be robbed of the opportunity to understand what's appropriate and what's not. Just as a child needs to know that there are boundaries and that some behavior is OK and some is not OK, so does your dog. He must understand the difference between right and wrong, too, and it is up to you to teach him this lesson. It is also your responsibility to get the message across in a nonabusive way.

I think that the majority of owners who have bought into the concept of "no correction" training suffer from a misconception about the word *correction*, so let me give you my definition. Let's say I am talking, and you are teaching me a phrase. You say the phrase; I begin to repeat it to you. You interrupt me to tell me that I mispronounced a word. I start the phrase over and this time pronounce the word correctly. What just happened was that you

Children and dogs need to grow up understanding right and wrong.

simply *corrected* me, and I repeated the phrase and got the word right on the second try. That is all a correction is. In not correcting your dog, you are confusing him. He will never understand what you want, and he will never know right from wrong.

There are parts of this technique that might work well for Blue, Green, or some Yellow dogs, for certain behaviors, but what about the others? For instance, food is usually used as a reward. But this is not a good idea with a Red dog. If you already have a problem with a dog's being out of control, you don't want to push him even further in that direction. Your goal is to calm and to control the dog. With Red dogs, as I have said, you want to use a tactile reward (petting, play), not food.

As discussed in other chapters, depending on the color of dog you are training, the right type of correction to use varies immensely. With almost all of the dogs, the correction you give may be nothing more than simply asking the animal to repeat the behavior until it is performed correct-

## WRONG REWARD

People who use the "no correction" method usually make another mistake: consistently using only a food reward when training their dog. When using *only* a food reward, a few things are very likely to happen:

- You have an overexcited dog. As you have learned, treats and food rewards are not advised with Red and Orange dogs because it elevates their energy level.
- You have made your own actions predictable, opening yourself up to the possibility that your dog will begin to "test" you in an attempt to manipulate *your* behavior. If this happens, you might find the training relationship uncomfortably reversed.
- You have no way to guide the animal's behavior if something is done incorrectly. What if the dog has the bad habit of lunging away from you while he is on the leash? What if you have a problem with the dog running out the door? How do you correct the animal if you use only a food reward?

Using a technique that involves *no corrections* with a high-energy Orange dog such as this one would be nearly impossible.

ly. With a Red dog, this may also involve gently manipulating the animal back into position.

## THE "ALPHA DOG"

Before I begin, I must mention that I know some great dog trainers, including professional trainers for police departments and other law enforcement agencies, who have been extremely successful using techniques built upon understanding and exploiting the dog's natural "pack" instinct. However, I will also tell you that during my thirty years of training animals for movies, television shows, and commercials, I have not known one animal trainer in Los Angeles who uses anything close to this alpha/submissive technique.

This is an extremely complex style of training, and it is my belief that the average pet owner does not need to understand "pack" instinct in dogs unless he or she lives with three or more dogs. The biggest reason for this is that the dogs are living in *our* world; we are not living in their world. They are not wolves, coyotes, or other wild animals. Pack dynamics don't necessarily apply when working with individual dogs or small groups of dogs.

As dog owners, we put ourselves in total control by determining what will take place on a day-to-day basis—we determine specific times for training, meals, walks, play, and sleeping. This means that every one of us is an alpha whether or not we choose to display the so-called dominant behaviors of an alpha.

Furthermore, trainers can make many mistakes in trying to teach the "pack philosophy" to the average pet owner. One of the first messages they convey is that being alpha is the number one priority. In my opinion—and in the prevailing wisdom of the professional dog-training industry—this is 100 percent wrong. Instead of becoming alpha, the first thing that the average pet owner needs to do is develop a positive relationship with the new dog. The owner needs to build trust to ensure that the dog will genuinely want to be around him or her. A new pet owner can create many problems by neglecting to do this at the outset.

Some people who teach training techniques based on pack philosophy have even developed different "tests" that reportedly enable them to determine how alpha a dog is. One example is taking a rolled-up newspaper and raising an arm as if to hit the dog, then seeing how the dog reacts. Hmm, what do you think the average dog would do if he didn't know you and it looked as if you were going to hit him with something? His natural instinct probably will be to respond in one of two ways: try to run away, or try to bite you. There is also a slim possibility that the dog will just stay there. Then there is another variable—the animal's unknown history. If a new pet comes from an animal shelter and his previous history is unknown, it's possible that the dog was seriously harmed by an action like this in the past. Based on the response of the dog, the assumption would be that he's a "fear biter" (if he tries to back off, run away, or bite to get away) or "aggressive" (if he comes at the person and tries to bite or growls).

So, basically, either way you have a "problem dog," right? Wrong!

Some do another "test" by putting the dog on his back and basing everything on how the dog responds. I don't think you can judge a dog's personality based on how the dog reacts. Dogs are like people, and some can be very pleasant but just don't like to be put on their backs.

Another thing I have heard that I find totally ridiculous is that you should never let your dog be higher than you in elevation. This means that if your dog is on the couch and you are on the ground, it is wrong, because you are not in the alpha position. Some believers in the pack philosophy also think you should always go through a door before the dog. In my opinion, having a dog should be a fun thing. Many times, training based in pack philosophy is based on almost scaring the new owners and immediately putting them on the defensive with their dogs, when they should really be focusing on that bond. At this time it is essential that a new owner start with a positive, rather than a negative, approach.

This dog clearly has no problem being put on his back, but many dogs really dislike it, and whether your dog will let you manipulate him this way tells you little about how to train him.

I think it is so much easier when the average pet owner understands how to coexist with the dog and that the dog just wants to please him or her. If owners use the alpha/submissive technique, especially on a Blue, Green, or Yellow dog, they could easily destroy the dog's trust in them very quickly. Beliefs based on so-called universal truths about dog behavior may have little basis in the reality of *your* dog's situation in *your* household. Putting these beliefs into practice and attempting to assert your "alpha" status can result in real damage to the bond you are attempting to build with your dog. Adherence to accepted notions of "pack philosophy" may prevent you from seeing your dog as an individual with specific needs that could be addressed more successfully in a custom-tailored training program such as mine.

## CLICKER TRAINING

If there's anything owners can do to establish better relationships with their dogs, they should always do it. If you have a Blue, Green, or Yellow dog and the only thing that makes sense to you is clicker training, then by all means employ this technique. This can really work when the owner or the trainer is looking to motivate the dog and to increase his energy level. One of the most popular settings for this is in agility training. But as I've said before, I do not recommend clicker training for Red or Orange dogs (see page 89).

As far as basic training goes, there are other methods you can use that will keep the animal under better control. Clicker training was actually developed many years ago; today it is a very common and quite successful technique used in theme parks and oceanariums with marine mammals. I used it many years ago in the training of dolphins, sea lions, and orcas and still use it, although rarely, in dog training.

### How Clicker Training Works

There are different ideas about how clicker training should work. To understand my style of clicker training, you need to know what a click actually represents to marine mammals. A click or a whistle in marine-mammal training signals a bridge, which is the amount of time between when the animal hears a sound and when the animal is rewarded.

This technique is popular in marine-mammal training because most interactions with marine mammals happen at such long distances. It is a great way, and really the only way, of letting the animal know he did something correctly when the trainer is 30 or 40 feet away. Here is how it works:

- An orca performs an incredible jump out of the water.
- The trainer blows the whistle, letting the whale know he did the jump correctly.
- The whale hears the whistle and understands that what he did at that *exact second* was correct.
- Between the time the whale hears the whistle and the time he returns to the trainer, he is still registering that what he did was correct.
- When the whale reaches the trainer, he receives his reward.

Many of the techniques I use today with the clicker are derivatives of the techniques I used twenty-five years ago with killer whales such as Shamu.

The marine mammals I've trained did not always get a treat after each correctly performed behavior, but they knew when they did something right.

A sea lion raising his flipper offers another fine example. As soon as the flipper reaches a certain height, the trainer clicks. *It is a defined sound at a defined time.* It works great in these types of situations. Now, let's fast-forward to dog training.

When you talk to some of the people who have recently been taught about clicker training, the first thing they will say is, "I click and feed . . . click and feed." If you click and feed repeatedly, what is the animal doing after you click? If I am constantly clicking and feeding, is the dog watching me or watching what's in my hands? Over the course of time, he will learn to look at my left hand as I click, and then his eyes will go directly to my right hand, looking for the food reward. The dog isn't paying attention to *me* but to a part of me—the hand with the treat. Regardless of the dog I am training, the last thing I want is for the dog to be focused anywhere but on me.

If we go back to marine-mammal training, the whistle did not necessarily mean "food is coming"; it was instead an affirmation that the action the animal just performed was correct. If you watch the actions of some of the best marine-mammal trainers out there, you'll see that they don't *always* feed the animal when he does something correctly. They use different types of rewards, and sometimes they will simply send the animal on to the next behavior. This way, the trainer does not become predictable. The variation keeps the animal guessing, keeping training stimulating and fun.

You will see the same thing happen with agility training because the reinforcement builds attitude and motivation and increases the animals' energy levels. When you consistently give the same food reward to a whale or a dolphin at the same intervals, you become predictable; this can happen in dog training.

## Which Colors Click

In basic dog training I have seen that the constant clicking and feeding can actually have the same effect it does in marine-mammal training and get the dog even more excited. That's great if you are training your dog in agility or want to increase the dog's energy level. However, in most training especially in the early training of Red and Orange dogs, a more excited dog is the last thing the owner wants. I would say that at least 60 percent to 70 percent of dogs that people train are initially Orange or Red. These are relatively high-strung and very high-spirited dogs with a great deal of energy. Most owners of these dogs want to calm them down, not get them fired up. Thus, I certainly would not recommend using clicker training with Orange dogs or Red dogs.

However, Blue or Green dogs need to get excited and motivated. Although I teach different ways to do that, clicker training may be a good alternative for these animals.

## FORCE VERSUS MANIPULATION

Trust develops from a process of incorporating yourself into your dog's life in a positive way. The time you have spent together has ensured that your dog simply wants to be with you. As you continue, you do not want to do anything to jeopardize everything you have just created.

Some of the older styles of obedience training involve a little bit of force; others involve a lot of force. Like anything, some people take it to more of an extreme than others do. By compelling your dog into situations and positions that are uncomfortable for him, yelling at him, hitting him, or over-correcting him using the chain collar, you risk not only hurting him but also obliterating your positive relationship and shattering his trust in you.

My training technique, which I call the Companions for Life Training Technique, is based on manipulation rather than compulsion. There is a huge difference. When you manipulate an animal into a position, your hands touch the dog gently and your voice is low and soothing. If you use a chain collar, the corrections are minimal. You will find that this technique works best with Red dogs, Orange dogs, and some Yellow dogs.

## Companions for Life Training Technique

I have put together this technique over the course of thirty years of dog training. It is a combination of many different techniques, including marine-mammal training. There are a few points I want you to remember as you train your dog:

- Keep the training sessions short, between 2 and 5 minutes.
- Before you take the your dog out and begin to train him, have a goal in mind of what you want to accomplish in the session. Make it a small goal. When you achieve that goal, end the session.
- During the session, give your dog his cue only once. A major reason owners have communication problems with their dogs is that they give multiple cues, which can cause confusion.
- End the session on a positive note. Do something your dog likes, such as tossing him a ball or giving him a treat, taking him for a walk, or just petting him. It makes the training session that much more rewarding. By consistently having fun after the training session, your dog will

understand that when he does what you want, the reward will come that much sooner.

- Remember that when you reward your dog, you should use as many types of rewards as possible. This is why a Yellow dog is ideal to work with; he might like a treat, a ball, or a toy. Remember, change is always reinforcing to your dog.
- When your dog does something incorrectly, you should always use the same correction. By using different corrections, you've introduced a change, and your corrections can actually be perceived as rewarding or reinforcing.

## Cuing, Rewarding, Correcting, and Releasing

All dog training comprises four actions: cuing, rewarding, correcting, and releasing. Mastering these skills is a large part of what makes a good dog trainer. Everyone has the ability to be a good dog trainer.

First, a good trainer must be able to give a very clear, single cue to the dog. One of the reasons there is a great deal of breakdown in behavior is that many dog owners give several different cues to their dogs without realizing they have done so. If there are different or numerous cues given, the animal

Whichever cue you give your dog, resist the impulse to repeat yourself.

## THE FOUR STEPS

It is important to understand the sequence of events that happens each time you ask the animal to perform a behavior. Start off by giving your dog a cue, initiating the chain of events. Your response to what your dog does when you ask him to perform a behavior is an important factor in the animal's learning that behavior. There should be only four events that will happen when you ask a dog to perform a behavior:

### 1. CUE

You will give the dog a cue. This could be either a visual cue (using your hand) or a verbal cue (using a spoken command).

### 2. THE RESPONSE

After you give the dog the cue, your dog will respond in one of two ways. The response will be either correct or incorrect. (Pretty simple so far—right?)

### 3. REWARD OR CORRECT

Based on the response, it is up to you to either reward the dog for doing the behavior correctly or correct the animal for doing the behavior incorrectly.

### 4. THE RELEASE

If the animal does the behavior correctly and you are content with the situation, release the dog. Remember, just because you rewarded the dog does not mean the sequence is over. The end of the sequence is dictated by you, not your dog, and that comes from your releasing him.

becomes confused and does not get a clear picture of what the owner wants him to do. But if the owner is consistent and gives the same cue repeatedly, training becomes much easier.

Second, a good trainer must be able to give the dog the most reinforcing thing that the animal likes when he does something correctly. Training according to colors plays a big role here. You need to make sure that you've taken enough time to identify the things your dog likes. My suggestion is to give your dog those things only when he does something correctly. Think about it from your perspective. If you knew that every once in a while, if you worked a little harder that week, there would be a check for $1,000 in your mailbox, wouldn't you always work a little harder?

Third, a good trainer must be able to look at a situation, know why an animal performed a particular behavior incorrectly, and give the most appropriate correction for that dog. Remember that correcting the animal is not necessarily giving a physical correction. This concept will be discussed in chapter 9, "Confusion and Testing."

Finally, a good trainer must be able to release the dog correctly. I don't believe enough dog trainers teach new pet owners the importance of this step. Often I see a new owner teaching the dog to sit and stay, and all goes well early on, but as soon as the owner rewards the dog, the dog gets up. If you think about it from his point of view, the dog just got up on his own and dictated when it was appropriate to get up. If the owner allows this to happen consistently, the dog will get up on his own more and more. Once this happens, the owner loses control of the dog's other behaviors in the training sessions. Trust me, dogs are smart. A smart dog that gets up consistently before he is released will only learn to try it over and over again. Simply put, you lose control and the dog wins.

Release is using a defined word and defined action to let the dog know "we are done"—this is something you are dictating, not the dog. What I have always done from the beginning is use the word *OK* with a firm and distinct pat on the dog's side area. Now he is released from that behavior. Afterward, you have the choice of what you do. But feel free to use whatever word or gesture you like!

Remember, all you are doing is *releasing* the animal from the previous behavior, and it is an excellent method for keeping control of the training situation.

# Confusion and Testing

**D**o you ever wonder why your dog does things incorrectly? Animals are going to be wrong sometimes. It's all part of learning—that is why I dedicated a whole chapter to it. One of the most important things to understand is why your dog will *not* do what you want him to do when you give him a cue. There are really only two possible explanations:

- He is confused (meaning that he truly does not know what you want).
- He is testing you (meaning that he knows what you want; he's just trying to get away with something).

Responding to a confused dog as if he is testing you will only lead to further confusion on his part. Responding to a dog that really is testing you will only lead to further testing on his part. So it is critical that you distinguish between the two.

## CONFUSION

The animal isn't being defiant; he simply does not understand what you want. This might happen for a number of reasons, but the biggest one is that the owner has progressed too quickly in the training of that specific behavior. For example, let's say you have just trained your dog to stay in the last few days, and the dog is very consistent when you are 2 feet away. Every time you get 2 feet away and tell him to stay, he stays. But in this training session you go from 2 feet away to 8 feet away. As you are asking him to stay, he keeps getting up and walking toward you. Is this testing or confusion? Let's look at it from his perspective:

* He just learned to stay only a few days ago.
* He was very consistent from 2 feet away, but all of a sudden you move to 8 feet away, and that's when the problems start.
* Because he just learned this behavior and has been doing well until the change of one variable, it is probable that the dog is honestly confused.

## TESTING

The animal knows how to do the behavior; he's just trying to get away with something. Why would your dog do this after you have developed an awesome relationship? Actually, it's not such a bad thing. It's the sign of a smart dog, and it's something that very intelligent animals often do. How do you know when a dog is testing you? Let's look at the example again. You have just trained your dog to stay in the last few days, and the dog is consistently staying from 2 feet away. Today you brought him out as usual and asked him to stay from 2 feet away again; you made no changes. But this time, he got up and started walking toward you. If there are no distractions, then there is a good chance that the dog is not staying because he is testing you. Think about it:

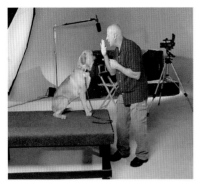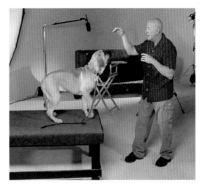

If the dog is consistent from this short distance and you move to 8 to 10 feet away too fast, you can really confuse the dog.

A dog that is staying from this distance for a week understands the behavior. If he suddenly isn't staying, then he is most likely testing you.

- He just learned to stay from 2 feet away only a few days ago.
- He was very consistent in the past few days.
- You did not do anything different today, and there were no distractions.

## UNDERSTANDING AND CORRECTING

It is essential that you understand *why* your dog did the behavior incorrectly. In most cases, if the animal is honestly confused, it is because something the trainer did confused the animal. You need to know why your dog did something incorrectly because the ways you correct him for testing you or for being confused are as different as night and day.

### Correcting for Confusion

If you are correcting the animal for confusion, remember that he was confused and did not know what you wanted. You will see this in dogs of all colors but more frequently in Blue dogs. The way you correct the animal is to *make the command easier to understand*. Remember, the dog was great at 2 feet away for a few days. Then you tried to get him to stay from 8 feet away and had problems. Here's how to correct him:

1. Go back to where the animal was the most consistent—only 2 feet away.

2. Once the animal is consistently staying from 2 feet away, move to 3 feet away (not 8).

3. Once the animal is consistently staying from 3 feet away, move 4 feet away (and so on).

All we are doing is going a little slower and making it easier for your dog to comprehend.

## Correcting for Testing

If you are correcting the animal for testing you, remember that the animal understood how to do the behavior and was doing it wrong on purpose. You will see this more with Red, Orange, and Yellow dogs and a lot less frequently with Blue or Green dogs. The way you correct the animal for testing you is to *make him repeat the behavior*. Remember that the dog knew what you wanted in the first place. Let's consider the following scenario as an example:

1. You told him to stay from 2 feet away and he was testing you. Bring him back to the same place and make him stay. If he gets up, tell him to sit, and make him stay.

2. You might want to be a little closer so you can correct him more quickly if he gets up.

3. If he gets up, immediately tell him to sit and stay.

4. Once he is consistently staying from 2 feet away for the desired amount of time, you may reward him.

5. As you can see, we never made it easier. When correcting for an animal testing you, he must understand that *you (the trainer) are the boss.*

## MISREADING YOUR DOG

The biggest reason many dog owners have a breakdown in training is that they simply misread why their dogs did the behavior incorrectly. Can you imagine correcting a dog for being confused when he is actually testing you, or correcting a dog for testing you when he is confused? It happens. Let's look at our example again.

**If your dog starts testing you, take him back to his spot and remain close to him. Then if he gets up, you can immediately make him sit and stay.**

The dog was great at 2 feet away for a few days, which meant that he understood it pretty well from that distance. When you tried to get him to stay from 8 feet away, you had problems. There is a good chance that the dog was confused. Let's assume that you believed he was testing you; what would happen? Remember that the way you correct the animal for testing is to make him repeat the behavior. If you think about it, you would be making him repeat a behavior that he does not understand to begin with, which will create more confusion.

Let's say you just trained your dog to stay in the last few days, and the dog is very consistent with you being 2 feet away. Today, though, when you asked him to stay, he kept getting up and walking toward you. Since this is a behavior that the dog obviously understood for the past few days, there is a good chance that the dog is just testing you. Let's say the way you corrected the animal was for confusion, meaning you're now going to make it easier on him, so you adjust the distance. Remember that the correction for a dog that is testing you is to make him repeat the behavior—*not* to make it easier on him. Once your dog learns that he can test you and your response will be to accommodate him, I can guarantee you that he will try it with other behaviors down the road.

# Training Puppies

**T**his chapter is meant to help you with the training of your puppy. Other books are written specifically for puppy training, so I will keep it brief here. The purpose of this chapter is really to make you aware that you are training an immature animal and not an adult dog. There is a huge difference between puppies and grown dogs when it comes to training. I believe it is OK to train a puppy, as long as the training remains fun. If it is done the right way, the owner or trainer can really accomplish a lot, and training can be a great experience.

Dogs have incredible memories, retaining much of what they are taught, even at very early ages. That is why it is essential that you make training a positive practice for your puppy. To do this, I have always believed, you need to take two things into consideration: your puppy's age and his "color."

In general, the younger the puppy, the fewer corrections you are going to want to give him.

When dealing with a puppy, there is a fine line between correcting enough to get the message across and correcting too much. Remember that a correction might be nothing more than having the animal repeat the behavior. We always want to keep training an enjoyable experience for a young puppy.

The color of your dog is also a key factor. In general, if you have a Red puppy, you are training a rambunctious little ball of energy, and you can afford to give more corrections than if you were training a shy and timid Blue puppy.

When you combine age and color, you will get a better idea of what you are dealing with. Below are a few examples that I think will help you.

## RED AND ORANGE PUPPIES

Red and Orange puppies can be divided into two age groups for training purposes.

### Three to Five Months Old

Even though an Orange or Red puppy may be a little out of control, understand that it is still a very young dog. It's also

Be sure to give your new trainee plenty of time to play, explore, and just enjoy puppyhood.

# THE BOND

With my Companions for Life system, the focus is on building the relationship and trust with the animal early. Especially with a puppy, you need to take your time and establish that relationship prior to training. What many new pet owners find is that it's actually a lot easier to create this bond with a puppy than with an adult dog; puppies are so willing to be your friend.

There are many things you can do to help build a great bond with your puppy. Taking him for walks are some of the best times to really get to know the animal in addition to giving him exercise. Here are a few more tips:

- Once your puppy has had all his shots, take him with you to as many places as possible.
- Try to expose your puppy to as many distractions as possible. If there is something that you find that the puppy is a little afraid of or unsure of, take the time to get him comfortable with it.
- Identify the things the puppy likes and dislikes. If there is a certain treat that the puppy likes, try to remember and use that in your training sessions.
- As quickly as a bond can be built, it can be torn apart just as easily. An owner's consistent negative responses to a particular behavior problem can seriously jeopardize the relationship with your puppy. Instead of trying to punish him, try to come up with ways of not giving him the opportunity to be in those situations or environments in the first place.

You have the ability to form an awesome bond with your puppy. If this is done the right way and you make it fun, you will be amazed at what an incredible foundation this will lay for subsequent training.

very important that the puppy be able to play and do the things that puppies do. From what I have seen, if there is a time that mistakes are made with the training of puppies, it is with *this color puppy at this age*. The biggest mistake is not letting the puppy play and just be a puppy. Although I would recommend using chain collars on most Orange or Red dogs, I would *not* recommend using one on a puppy of this age.

For the reward of a little treat, this pup is enthusiastic about almost *anything*.

One of the problems I often see is overcorrecting. It doesn't have to necessarily be a physical correction, either. Sometimes constantly telling an Orange or Red puppy at this young age that his behaviors are wrong can make the training session an unpleasant experience. Once training is no longer an enjoyable experience, the dog no longer looks forward to being trained. It is essential that you make training fun. One of the ways this is accomplished is by using treats or something the dog likes to guide the animal into the position you want.

A great example is using the same technique I recommend for training the Blue dog in chapter 6—using a treat reward. Think about guiding the puppy into behaviors instead of forcing him. This makes the training 100 percent positive. At this point, keep everything fun and *be patient*.

## Six to Twelve Months Old

If this is a dog that you just recently purchased or rescued, I am sure you have a handful of puppy right now. Even so, at this age your Red puppy is going to require a lot of patience on your part. I do not recommend using a chain collar to train most puppies, but with *this color puppy at this age I do.* Review chapter 7 to help you understand the right and wrong ways to put a chain collar on the dog and use it correctly.

Depending on the size of the six-month-old Orange or Red puppy you are training, you may need to give more of a physical correction. For instance, you might be dealing with a very out-of-control Lab that is already 50 pounds. Obviously you may need to be a little more physical with him than with a 20-pound puppy. Just be smart when using the chain collar. If there are any physical corrections involved in the session, make sure you follow the training session with something positive, such as playing with the puppy and his favorite toy.

If treats or food can be incorporated without the puppy's getting too unruly, definitely use them. You want to always use all of the positive methods you can.

Look at chapter 4 and follow the techniques that I recommend for training Yellow dogs, too. With that technique, you will find that there are some aspects that come from training Orange and Red dogs and others that come from training Green and Blue dogs.

## YELLOW PUPPIES

The good news is you have a Yellow puppy. What's even better is that, as mellow as this puppy is, he will only mellow more with age. Whether your Yellow puppy is three or twelve months old, if you make training fun, you can accomplish a lot behaviorally.

**Yellow puppies are a pleasure to start training at a young age; remember to keep it fun for them.**

What you will find is that almost all Yellow puppies, like the Yellow adults, will look to you for guidance. I have had a great deal of fun training these types of dogs at a young age, and you would not believe some of the things that I have trained. If it is done the right way and you keep it fun, you will be amazed at the behaviors you can train, too.

What's also great about most Yellow puppies is that once they start to learn behaviors, they really seem to enjoy the accomplishment. If you are looking to perk them up, you will find that certain foods or treats do the job well. At the same time, if you are looking to calm the dog down, sometimes just your voice is enough to have an impact.

For the training of Yellow puppies, take a look at chapter 8 and follow the type of training techniques that are used with the Green or Blue dog. This method deals with guiding the animal into positions like sitting and staying. Because this technique follows the same guidelines as the training of the Green or Blue dog, I would not recommend using a chain collar on a Yellow puppy.

**Your timid Blue or Green puppy needs more time and patience in training than do his warmer-colored counterparts.**

## BENJI: A GREEN PUPPY

Many dogs I have trained that started out as Green or Blue puppies became animal actors and great working dogs. Frank Inn (shown here with Benji), the late, great trainer and owner of the two dogs who played "Benji" (their real names were Higgins and Benji), would have told you that Benji, were she still alive, would be a Green dog—and to this day one of the best dogs ever to work in the film and television industries.

## BLUE OR GREEN PUPPIES

There are just a few important things to remember when training Green or Blue puppies, and it doesn't really matter what age they are. Whether you are training a three-month-old or a ten-month-old, be patient and try to make training a fun and enjoyable experience.

Within the first thirty days of having your puppy, I am sure you will find different types of treats that he likes. I am also sure you'll notice some things that the puppy is afraid of. You want to make sure that you incorporate the things the puppy likes into the training session. And you should try to eliminate those things the puppy does not like. Get rid of the distractions so he can focus more on you and the training session.

You want to follow the technique that is used in chapter 6 for training the Blue dog. This technique will require you to guide the animal into behaviors such as sitting and staying; it will not require the use of a chain collar. You will find that using the collar your puppy normally wears will be sufficient.

The one thing you want to do with all puppies, especially Green and Blue ones, is perfect your patience. The good news is that the best time to deal with any fears or uncertainties that this puppy might have is in the beginning, so you are training your dog at a great time.

# Learning to Train Using the Sit/Stay

I n this chapter, you will learn how to train. I will teach you the basic steps using the *sit/stay* command. Much of what you learn here can be used in teaching the other commands. In the following chapters, I focus on each command, using the proper mannerisms, corrections, and rewards for your color dog

Before you begin the actual training of the sit/stay behavior, I recommend that you take your dog out for a pretraining session. I encourage new pet owners to pretrain because doing so gives them a chance to know their dogs better and to familiarize themselves and their dogs with the tools they will be using.

In this chapter, I talk about two different styles for pretraining and training dogs to sit/stay. One of them is used for the Red and Orange dogs; the other one is used for the Yellow, Green, and Blue dogs.

## RED AND ORANGE DOGS

As I have said in previous chapters, because of their high-energy, high-strung personalities, Red and Orange dogs need to be calmed and anchored during their training. That begins with preparations in pretraining.

### Pretraining Your Red or Orange Dog

Before beginning training, there is a certain exercise that I like to have owners go through with their high-strung dogs. It's great because it really involves no training of an actual behavior but teaches your dog a little control and helps you get comfortable with the dog, the leash, and the chain collar.

Go back to chapter 7 and look again at how to put a chain collar on your dog. I cannot stress enough the importance of doing this properly, as I've found that many people start off training on the wrong foot. Take your time and study the proper way to use a chain collar so you can keep the corrections to a minimum and also ensure that the tool is effective.

Here is one if the first mistakes that many new dog owners make when using the chain collar: they let the dog wander a few feet away from them before they actually correct him. They might even let their dogs lunge 3 to 5 feet away before they take action.

One of the biggest reasons people develop behavior problems with their dogs is simply that they send mixed messages, and this is one of the very first ones. Think about it from the dog's point of view. If he lunges or wanders and gets corrected at 3 to 5 feet away from you, what did he get corrected for, and does he know it? Was he lunging at 2 feet, 3 feet, or 4 feet away?

If you consider the laws of physics, the farther away from you that your dog is, the harder you need to pull on the leash to correct him. Some people simply do not have the strength

OPPOSITE: When the dog is this far in front of you, he can be very confused about the reason you are correcting him.

to correct their dogs from 4 or 5 feet away. If you are a very strong person, it could also injure your dog if you correct vigorously from 4 or 5 feet away.

Here's the way you eliminate those problems! Using the chain collar and a 6-foot leash, proceed by taking the following steps:

1. Put the chain collar on your dog and attach the leash the way it was shown in chapter 7.
2. Position your dog on your left side facing forward, as if you were going to be walking with your dog, but just stand in one place.
3. It doesn't matter if the dog sits or stands on all fours. The most important thing is that the dog is right next to you in a stationary position.
4. It is very important to keep the dog's nose behind your leg, next to your leg, or a few inches in front of your leg.
5. Keep some slack in the leash.
6. With the dog right next to you, if he does lunge away or begins to pull, you will correct him.
7. Because you are so close to the dog, you will use a very light, minimal correction that almost anyone can give. Remember, the closer the dog is, the easier it is on you

Having tension in the leash will make correcting your dog more difficult—harder for you and harder on him.

When the dog is in this position, he understands the correction.

and him. You do not need to say "No." Let the chain collar do all the talking.

8. Now you have shown your dog that if he moves or lunges only a few inches, he is corrected. I think this is an important part of Red dog training because it sends a very clear and distinct message of what you expect from *day one*.

9. After you correct him, feel free to pet the dog very gently and talk to him in that same manner.

Having slack in the leash is very important. If there is *no* slack, there is constant pressure, and the dog will only learn to pull and will never learn just to stand or sit there. This is something that will become conditioned. Now that you are aware of this, you will begin to notice it with many pet owners and their dogs, and it's something that most of them are totally unaware of. When you get to the point where the dog is either sitting or standing there with slack in the leash, you are making great progress.

Rewarding your dog promptly and properly is also critical. The dog will learn that if he either sits or stands next to you and is relaxed, he will be rewarded by your petting him. However, if he lunges or moves a few inches from the position, he will be corrected.

It is very important to understand that most Red dogs want attention. By going through this pretraining process, you've made things simpler. He will understand that in order to receive the tactile rewards that he most likely wants, he must stay in control next to you and, most important, not pull.

I believe this is a critical exercise to go through at the very beginning, so make sure you take your time. If you feel that you want to spend a few extra days with this before you proceed with training, feel free to do so. Remember, all dogs are different, and some will need more time than others will.

By using this technique, you will lay a great foundation for all the behaviors that appear later in this book. To recap, you've learned how to properly put a chain collar on your dog as well as how to properly use it. Now that you've learned that you *don't* have to yank on it, you've made things easier on yourself and, more important, easier on your dog.

Once you have done this for a day or two and your dog is consistently staying next to your left side without pulling on the leash, you are now ready to begin with the first behavior, the sit/stay.

## Teaching Your Red or Orange Dog to Sit/Stay

There are two different ways to teach the sit/stay: with treats and without treats.

The first way is done with no manipulation at all. You simply guide the dog into the sitting position by using a treat. This is the technique that is used in training Blue, Green, Yellow, and Yellow-leaning Orange dogs. It is 100 percent positive and does *not* involve manipulating the dog. I would not recommend this technique with Red dogs or

## SIT/STAY—GENTLE MANIPULATION

I always like to train sitting and staying at the same time. One reason is that from the beginning your dog understands to stay each time he is told to sit. By training both at once, it gives you an incredible amount of control and makes the training of other behaviors much easier.

Another reason I train these behaviors first is that they are the simplest for the dog to understand. It is nearly impossible for the dog to cheat, or move from the sitting and staying position, without getting up.

with Red-leaning Orange dogs. If you think that your Orange dog would do fine with this method, then go to page 120.

The second way is done by using gentle manipulation, and with this method, you are simply positioning the animal into the sit. With this technique, understand that you will not be *forcing* the dog, just manipulating him. This is the technique you will use with Red and some Orange dogs.

### PREPARATION

The first thing you want to do is position the dog at a higher elevation than the ground where you are standing. So you might want to train your dog on your porch, a step, a table, or maybe even a curb.

Have a leash attached to the chain collar just as you did during pretraining. Make sure the leash is attached properly. You probably will not be correcting your dog much with the chain collar, but it's a good idea to keep it on while training.

### PHASE 1

Guide your dog onto the elevated area. Once he gets up there, give him a tactile reinforcement (petting him in his favorite spot). He should be a little calmer on the leash since you've spent a few days getting him used to it.

**Petting your dog on an elevated area can have a positive and calming effect.**

Once he is in a position facing you and in your control, drop the leash. Make sure that if your high-strung dog jumps off the elevated area at any time, which is likely to happen with your Red friend, you grab the leash and guide the dog back into the proper position. This will teach him that this is the place that he needs to be.

When the dog is in the position that you like and he is calm, put one hand on his chest. Talk to the dog softly as you do this. Put the other hand on the dog's rear end, at the base of his tail.

When you feel that you have some control, say "Sit," and as you do, manipulate the dog backward by applying downward pressure from your hand at the base of the tail area. At the same time, you can help by pushing the dog backward with the hand you have on his chest. (See page 118.)

Because both hands move together, this becomes almost a type of backward rocking motion.

When the dog gets into the sitting position, immediately say "Stay" while holding your hand in the air.

If the dog stays for a few seconds, use a tactile reward right away. Then give him the release, saying "OK," and let him get up.

Many owners make a major mistake by not teaching the dog to stay at this point. If he is not told to stay, he will probably just get up on his own, and the last thing

Make sure the leash is attached to the chain collar correctly.

you want to do early on in training is lose control over his actions. By teaching your dog to stay when you teach him to sit, you retain control.

This is the sequence of events:

1. Say "Sit."
2. Gently manipulate the dog into the sitting position.
3. Immediately say "Stay."
4. Release the dog.

Did you have a problem somewhere? I will help you!

Did your dog get up after you made him sit, or did he jump off the elevated area? Make sure that if your dog does make a mistake, you do not make a big issue out of it. Here are some things you do *not* want to do.

- Do not say "No."
- Do not yell at your dog.
- Do not yank your dog.
- Do not hit your dog.

This is really a trademark of my technique. If you have a problem with your dog getting off the elevated area, the

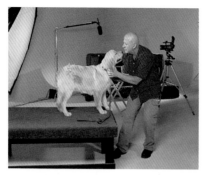

If your dog jumps off of the elevated area, patiently and gently guide him back up so he understands he must remain there.

When you are ready to begin training the *sit* command, place one hand on the chest of your dog.

For the next step, you will place the other hand on the dog's lower back, near the base of the tail.

With both hands in position, apply downward pressure with the hand on the dog's rear and, at the same time, gently push the dog's chest back.

way to correct him is by quietly guiding him back to the spot with the leash and repeating the behavior that you are working on.

If the dog keeps getting up every time you get him in the sitting position, consistently and gently manipulate the dog back into the sitting position—each time he gets up. It is imperative that you make him stay in that position for a moment. After that moment, you want to make sure that you say "Stay" and reward the dog. Make sure that you take very small steps so that you make this easy for your dog to understand. And be patient!

## PHASE 2

You will now begin fading out the gentle manipulation so that your dog begins to respond *only* to your verbal and visual cues.

**This is a visual cue for your dog to stay.**

Do you feel as if you don't need to keep a hand on your dog's chest or you don't need to manipulate as hard when he sits? If so, that is a good thing and means he's starting to understand what you want.

You'll find that very soon all you have to do is barely touch his back area as you say "Sit," and he will sit. That's great, because you are making more progress. Remember to say "Stay" as well, and then release him as you have always done.

This is really the point where everything starts making more sense to your dog. You will soon find that just as you go to touch your dog and say "Sit," he sits. That's great, because he sat *before* you touched him. When he responds and makes that progress, be sure to immediately reward him.

Look at the figures below, and notice that the hand cue to sit resembles the movement of your hand guiding him into the sitting position.

**Take a few minutes to practice the *sit* cue before giving it to your dog. Cup your hand, and move it in a downward arc.**

You can see that the dog is now starting to sit before my hand touches his back.

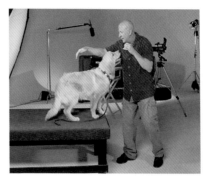

The hand is not even close to touching the dog; he is taking the cue entirely on his own.

The final phase is moving the dog onto the ground and then stepping 4 to 5 feet away from him.

Once your dog is consistently taking the cue from a few inches away, in the next sessions, he will probably respond to the cue when your hand is held a little farther away. This could be as much as 6 to 12 inches away as you say "Sit."

Once you've made this progress, you'll find that your dog is likely to start responding to the visual cue from as much as a foot away from his rear end.

You can see how this plays out. Once the dog responds to the cue consistently from a foot away, you can move to 3 feet away, 4 and 5 feet away, and so on. Once this happens, you are ready for the final phase of the behavior.

The final phase of this behavior is to stand straight and give your dog the visual cue. Did he sit? If he did, congratulations! You just trained your dog to sit!

## YELLOW, GREEN, AND BLUE DOGS

For the training of sit/stay with Yellow, Green, and Blue dogs, you will find that you do not need nearly as much preparation as you would with Red dogs and Orange dogs.

## Pretraining Your Yellow, Green, or Blue Dog

In the following pages, you will see that training takes place on an elevated area. Blue and some green dogs may be a little uncomfortable up there in the beginning. If your dog shows discomfort, be patient and help him get used to the the area. Take him up there, then kneel beside him and pet him. Once he seems more comfortable, begin the training.

## Teaching Your Yellow, Green, or Blue Dog to Sit/Stay

The technique used in training Blue, Green, Yellow, and Yellow-learning Orange dogs is done with no manipulation at all. You simply guide the dog into the sitting position by using a treat. It is 100 percent positive.

### PREPARATION

Use an elevated surface to train your dog to sit. If it's a small dog, this could be anything from a sturdy table to a couch or chair. Training will be easier and more relaxing for your dog and a lot easier on your back. If you're training a large dog, I still recommend getting him on something more elevated than where you are standing, even if it's only by 5 or 6 inches. A low porch works well.

I would also begin training your dog in the place where he is most relaxed, with the least number of distractions possible. This is very important, especially in training dogs that can be a little shy or timid. If he's more comfortable in the backyard or house, those are both great places to start.

I am sure you have found treats that your dog likes. Carry them in a little pouch during training.

### PHASE 1

First get the dog on the elevated area in a position where he is simply standing on all fours, facing you. Initially, you want to just get the dog relaxed by petting him.

Now, take a treat out and give it to the dog. Very simple! After you give it to him, just pet him, making the area a positive place. You might even want to repeat this a few times.

At this point, I am just petting the dog and reassuring him. Do not rush this process.

Hold the leash with your left hand (or the right if you are left-handed).

In your right hand, hold a treat between thumb and forefinger.

Hold the treat about 2 to 3 inches above your dog's head.

Move the treat very slowly toward the back of your dog, keeping the treat at the same height.

The dog goes to sit as the treat moves above him.

In the beginning you want to take it very slowly with a Blue or Green dog. If you feel you need to talk to the dog or pet the dog to relax, certainly feel free to do so. You want the dog to feel comfortable taking the treat from your hand.

This time, holding the leash *lightly* with your left hand, take a treat between the thumb and index finger of your right hand so the dog can see it. Hold it about 2 or 3 inches over his head. Move it very slowly toward his tail, keeping the treat at the same height, and say "Sit."

In order for your dog to keep his eye on the treat as you move it toward his tail, he either will jump for it or—to keep it within sight—will have to sit.

When he sits, you want to immediately say "Stay" and hold your right hand in the air. This is the visual cue for your dog to stay. If he obeys, reward him with the treat, then release him. The mark of a good trainer is timing. Always reward the dog immediately when he completes a requested behavior.

If your dog did what you asked, say "Stay," then reward and release; if he tries to jump up for the treat, you will be able to prevent him from doing so by correcting with the leash. This is why I told you to put a leash on the dog. Remember that you are holding the leash in the hand opposite the one with which you feed your dog. Again, you want to have a little slack in the leash, keeping the hand holding the leash lower than your dog's head. As you repeat the process of holding the treat over your dog's head in the opposite hand, you will find that you now have some control. If your dog tries to jump up, you have the ability to control your dog and keep him from jumping. Your dog will figure out that when he jumps for the treat, he can't get off the ground. There is virtually no real physical correction because your dog never got the opportunity to complete the jump. After realizing that he can't get the treat, he should eventually sit. Just make sure you always have slack in the leash.

You want to repeat this process, making sure you always say "Sit" only one time, as you hold the treat over the dog's head and start moving it toward his tail.

As soon as he sits, remember to say "Stay" as you reward your dog. Then release him. Repeat this process three or four times.

When you have some consistency, end the session and have some fun with your dog. As you can see, sometimes the sessions will be very short, maybe only a minute or two! It is essential that Blue and Green dogs are having fun with this process.

## PHASE 2

The next thing we want to do is achieve some consistency. We want to know that every time we move the treat toward

**Here I simulate holding a treat over the dog's head.**

You can see what the cue actually looks like as the dog sits.

the back of the dog, the dog sits. Once that happens, you can proceed.

We want to start eliminating, or phasing out, the use of a treat moving toward the tail. Begin by holding the treat stationary over the dog's head and saying "Sit," looking as if you are going to move the treat toward his tail. When the dog sits, say "Stay," and reward the dog immediately. Your dog now understands that when you hold your hand over his head and you say "Sit," you want him to sit. Make sure that your dog is performing the sit consistently before you move on to the next step.

When you're ready to eliminate the treat, hold your hand in the same position over your dog's head. Say "Sit." It looks as if you are still holding the treat, doesn't it? Your hand position will actually become the dog's cue to sit. If your dog sits, again tell him "Stay" and then reward him.

You are now giving your dog the cue to sit and saying "Sit." If your dog sits consistently, congratulations! You just trained your dog to sit!

As the dog sits more and more consistently, you can start increasing the distance from which you give your cue.

# Training Your Dog to Stay

**W**hen teaching your dog the stay behavior, as when teaching him the sit behavior, you will find that it is not so much that the technique changes significantly based on the color of your dog; what changes are the ways that you act around your dog, reward him, and correct him. In the fol-
lowing pages, I will tell you how those three factors vary according to the per-sonality of a dog so you can utilize the most effective approach for your color dog. (That is, of course, what really sepa-rates my technique from others.) Once you have a good grasp of the appropriate mannerisms, rewards, and corrections, I will show you how to go about training your dog to follow the *stay* command.

## TEACHING YOURSELF TO TRAIN

To train your dog effectively, you must first learn *how* to train your particular dog. In other words, you need to train yourself to train. That involves three key factors:

- Your mannerisms (the way you move, talk, and touch)
- Rewards
- Corrections

Take a look at the table on the following pages, and read the material pertaining to your dog's color carefully; then return to this page to begin the training.

## TRAINING YOUR DOG TO STAY

Others issues involved in the training of the stay behavior include when to reward your dog, working in an elevated area, and time and distances.

### Rewarding

There's no question that one of the most common problems new dog owners have is getting their dogs to stay. A big reason for that is that they don't reward their dogs at the right time. For instance, an owner will tell his dog to stay and when the dog does so, he will call the dog to him *before* offering a reward.

Think about this from your dog's point of view. If you are rewarding him *after* you call him over, he thinks you're rewarding him for *coming*—and that is a whole different behavior (which I will show you in chapter 13). So if you consistently reward your dog for coming to you, why would he ever want to stay? This is why your dog needs to be rewarded while he's staying and in the exact place he's staying. Walk over there and reward him; don't ask him to come to you.

### Elevated Area

I want to talk about the elevated area where you have been training your dog to sit and stay. Whether you're training your dog on a chair, couch, table, porch, or another surface, it is a designated and defined place, and we use it to make things easier for your dog. When you're training your dog to stay on something elevated and you begin to back away, there's really only one mistake your dog is going to make: jumping off. Of course, when he makes that mistake, your response will be to bring him back to the elevated area and ask him to sit and stay again. It will be easy for him to realize that when he jumps off the elevated area, he will be brought back and asked to repeat the behavior, but when he stays, he will be rewarded. Once he's got that figured out, which do you think he'll rather do?

For this reason, I do not train my dogs to stay on flat ground. On flat ground, there is no designated training place, and it becomes very easy for your dog to cheat. He will do things such as scoot his rear end on the ground or maybe even start getting up and walking toward you.

If your dog got up and began walking toward you and you took him back to the area and repeated the behavior, what would your dog think he was being corrected for? He might think it was for:

- Getting up from the sit position.
- Getting up and walking 1 foot.
- Getting up and walking 3 feet toward you.

This can become very confusing for your dog and can make it harder for him to figure out what you are trying to teach. For this reason, I like to use the elevated area.

The great news is that most dogs catch on to this behavior pretty quickly after they have been trained to sit. Even some of the

An elevated area gives your dog a defined training space.

# TRAINING YOUR DOG TO SIT/STAY

## MANNERISMS

**R E D**

Since you may lack control early on, you might need to stay a little closer to your dog for a while. Don't try to progress too quickly.

You also may find that as you begin to put some distance between you and your dog, he may get a little excited. Often when a Red dog gets a little excited, he will "break his stay" (get up from that position). A great way to avoid this is to try to keep the dog calm.

As you are telling your Red dog to stay, don't be afraid to be a bit loud or a bit forceful in your tone of voice.

**O R A N G E**

Although this is a high-strung dog, you'll see that once most Orange dogs have learned to sit, it really begins to help calm them down (and move in the Yellow direction), and it lays an excellent foundation for the stay.

You might want to limit your movement in the beginning of training. If you find that your own movement is not an issue, proceed. You will find that this potential distraction within the controlled environment of the training situation will help you desensitize your dog to many distractions he may encounter in everyday life.

Don't be afraid to raise your voice if you have to.

Remember that as your Orange dog begins to calm down and turn Yellow, you will not have to be as loud or use as firm a tone.

**Y E L L O W**

The Yellow dogs pick up on the stay about as quickly as any other behavior. Once you have your Yellow dog staying from a short distance, you can be very animated in your expressions and movements. Your Yellow dog might really like this!

One of the great things about Yellow dogs is that they like a lot of variety. You and your dog can have a lot of fun with this behavior by changing things up.

You will also notice that as you are telling the Yellow dog to stay, you can speak softly. When you say "Stay," your voice should almost sound as if you are speaking calmly to another person.

## REWARDS

As you reward your Red dog for staying, make sure that he is rewarded for sitting and staying. The reason I say this is that the Red dog is the color most likely to jump up before you reward him.

Treats will probably add to your dog's excitement level, so instead you want to make sure you begin by using a tactile reward, such as petting your dog, each time he stays.

As for the sit behavior, always try spending some extra time petting your dog. By walking to your dog and rewarding him for staying, you not only send a positive message to your dog but also, in some cases, can have a calming effect on him.

With most Orange dogs, you can begin to incorporate a treat as you start training them to stay, but keep a close eye on your dog's reactions to food rewards. If you see that the treat makes him go bananas, use a tactile reward instead.

As you are rewarding your Orange dog for staying, take some extra time to pet him right where he is staying. This can have a very calming effect on many dogs.

Most Yellow dogs are happy staying in one place from the beginning, knowing that some type of reward will follow.

Some great ideas for rewarding Yellow dogs for staying involve variety. Sometimes use a treat; at other times, use a tactile reward.

Treats will probably add to your dog's excitement level, but this is a good thing because that excitement might make the training session more fun.

## CORRECTIONS

You will find that most Red dogs can be a little stubborn and may not want to stay for too long in the very beginning, so take your time. This will limit your corrections.

If you are telling your dog to stay and he gets up from the sitting position, in most cases the main correction will be making him repeat the behavior.

Remember that some Red dogs can be a little hardheaded in the beginning. You may have to make your dog repeat the stay behavior a few times until he really understands.

Once an Orange dog begins to understand the stay, he catches on fairly easily. If your dog does get up, you can correct him by just taking him back to the spot and making him repeat the behavior.

From what I have seen, most Yellow dogs rarely need a correction for the stay behavior because it really is so simple, especially if you are using an elevated area.

The standard correction for this type of dog is simply making him repeat the behavior.

## MANNERISMS

**G R E E N**

Although the Green dog may not have the shyness of a Blue dog, you don't want to rush adding distance between you and the dog. The great part about these dogs is that once you achieve a little distance and they achieve a little confidence, training can progress relatively quickly.

Like the Yellow dog, many Green dogs like a little variation in the routine. As the two of you grow comfortable, don't be afraid to shake things up a bit. Try moving around in different places to keep training interesting for the dog.

You will find with most Green dogs that you do not have to be loud when giving commands. In many instances, just the volume of your normal speaking voice will be sufficient.

**B L U E**

Because he may be extremely shy and timid, the Blue dog probably gets most of his security from being near you. This is why, as you begin to teach him to stay and start to develop some distance, you want to take it very slowly.

Once you do start to develop some distance, you might want to slowly begin to move around and stand in different places. This can make it interesting and fun for a dog with a Blue disposition and may better hold his attention.

Your voice is also key in teaching a dog like this to stay. With many Blue dogs, you don't need to raise the volume. Simply use your regular voice when giving him the command.

dogs toward the extremes of the spectrum, such as Red and Blue dogs, have now had a chance to "step out of their comfort zones."

When you are training your dog to sit using my technique, your are laying a solid foundation for training your dog to stay. Remember, you have said "Stay" each time you have told your dog to sit. By this time, your dog should already be sitting and staying for a few seconds on the elevated area with you standing right in front of him.

| REWARDS | CORRECTIONS |
|---------|-------------|
| The same reward that you used in teaching your Green dog to sit will apply to this behavior as well. Again, you will identify the most reinforcing treat that he likes and introduce that treat to him as you are teaching him to stay.<br><br>After you feed the dog a treat, feel free to spend some time petting him, too. Remember that any reward you give him for staying will always be taken as something positive. | The standard correction will be making the animal repeat the behavior. If your dog gets up from the staying position before you release him, make him repeat the behavior.<br><br>Make sure that fear is not the reason your Green dog is not staying. With these dogs, just be aware of what things may scare or startle them and keep them from staying. |
| The same reward that you used in teaching your Blue dog to sit will apply to this behavior as well. Again, you will identify the most reinforcing treat that he likes and introduce that treat to him during training.<br><br>After you feed the dog a treat, just keep petting him. Remember that any reward you give him for staying will always be taken as something positive. | The standard correction will be making the animal repeat the behavior.<br><br>If he gets up from the staying position before you release him, just make him repeat the behavior.<br><br>As with the Green dog, make sure the reason your dog is not staying isn't that he's afraid. Be aware that your voice or other factors in the training environment may scare or startle a Blue dog.<br><br>After some time, you will be amazed at how the Blue dog's confidence level really increases. |

## Time and Distance

When training your dog to stay, you want to think about two things: time and distance. Once you have your dog sitting and staying for a few seconds with some consistency, you can begin to slowly lengthen the distance at which he is doing so and increase the amount of time he holds the stay. This is really where you need to be creative and adapt your technique based on what you have observed of your individual dog's progress.

My suggestion is to train one thing at a time. Let's just start off with the amount of time your dog is staying.

## TIME

Start by setting some goals for yourself. If your dog is consistently staying for a few seconds, try to extend it to 5 seconds. If the dog is staying for 5 seconds consistently, the next day try for 10 seconds. Just increase it a little more each day, and always make sure you walk to your dog and reward him *while* he is sitting and staying. This is great for dogs that may be a little insecure in the beginning because it gives them the additional security of having you right there beside them.

If you train your dog with very short sessions over the course of a day or two, he should catch on pretty quickly. Keep in mind that during this stage we are focusing only on the time element. Once your dog is staying for 30 to 45 seconds consistently, you are ready to move on to the next step—distance.

## DISTANCE

Take your time with this part. A Blue or Green dog may be a little insecure when you step away from him. Once your dog is consistently staying from 1 foot away for a few sessions, try to back up and have the dog stay from 2 or 3 feet away. If that works, the next day try to move to 5 or 6 feet away.

 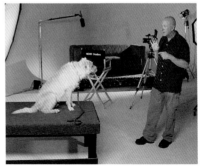

**Spend a lot of time building up to the distance of 2 to 3 feet away.**

**Eventually your dog will be staying from 6 to 8 feet away.**

For many Blue or Green dogs, the distance element will be much more of an issue than time is. For Red and Orange dogs, the time element is more of an issue because they just hate to sit still! With Yellow dogs, neither of the elements of the stay should really give you trouble.

Increase the distance a little more each day. Be sure to always walk to your dog and reward him for staying.

Once your dog becomes consistent with the distance element and is staying from about 10 feet away, you can begin to combine time and distance.

The next step might be a little challenging for your dog: eliminate the elevated area and move him to flat ground. You will find that because you have trained your dog on the elevated area for such a long period of time, you should have very few problems with his wanting to get up or cheat, especially if you are training a Yellow, Green, or Blue dog. It might take longer if you are training an Orange or Red dog.

Eventually you can start building your dog's sitting and staying on flat ground from a distance of 15 or 20 feet for a duration of 30 seconds. Once this happens, the behavior is really trained.

As your dog improves, don't be afraid to mix things up and have a little fun. If your dog is sitting and staying from 15 feet away, periodically reward him from only 4 or 5 feet away. If he is sitting and staying consistently for 30 seconds, every once in a while reward him after only 5 seconds. By doing this, you make it fun and interesting for your dog, and, most important, you do not become predictable.

Your dog has now learned to stay!

## Chapter 13

# Training Your Dog to Come

**T**here are many reasons why you need to teach your dog to come, but the biggest one is that you need to have control over your dog in any situation, particularly a potentially dangerous one. If your front door is open and your dog runs out, you need to know that he will come when you call him and not run into a busy street.

Half the battle in training your dog to come is making sure he wants to be with you as often as possible. You do that by building a great relationship with him before training starts (as I've said). If you have done so, then your dog will more readily respond when you call him.

There are some basic explanations for why a dog does not want to come when called:

- He sees another animal.
- He smells something interesting.
- He just doesn't want to be with you.

Remember that the animal always has a *choice*. His choice is to come to you or go in another direction. This is why this behavior is so much easier when you get yourself in a place with your dog where he likes you and wants to be with you.

In teaching your dog to come, much like in teaching him to stay and sit, you're going to find that the actual technique doesn't change much based on the color of your dog. What *will* change are the ways you act, reward your dog, and correct your dog. In the following pages, I will tell you how those three factors vary according to the personality of a dog so you can use the most effective approach for your color dog. (That is, as I've said, what really separates my technique from others.) Once you have a good grasp of the appropriate mannerisms, rewards, and corrections, I will show you how to go about training the *come* command.

## TEACHING YOURSELF TO TRAIN

To train your dog effectively, you must first learn *how* to train your particular color dog. In other words, you need to train yourself to train. That involves three key factors:

**Hold the long line at about the halfway point.**

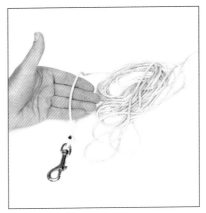

This standard 25- to 30-foot long line is available at many of your local pet stores.

This is one you can make with a small clip and some light line.

- Your mannerisms (the way you move, talk, and touch)
- Rewards
- Corrections

Review the table on the following pages, and study the material appropriate for your dog. Read carefully, and then return to this page to begin the training.

## TRAINING YOUR DOG TO COME

In training your dog to come, you must have the right tools and techniques for using them.

### An Important Training Tool

Before you train this behavior, you need to invest in an important tool, and that is a 30-foot line. You can find one of these at your favorite pet shop. If you have a dog that weighs less than 30 pounds, you might need to use the same length of leash but in something a little lighter, such as nylon.

The main reason you need to use this line is that your dog must understand that no matter where he is (whether he is 6 feet away or 25 feet away), he must come when you call him.

# TRAINING YOUR DOG TO COME

## MANNERISMS

**R**
**E**
**D**

Remember that if there is something or someone that your Red dog is interested in instead of coming to you, he will probably bolt fast. Make sure you are prepared for that.

As you teach your dog this behavior, you will be using a long line. Make sure that you are always holding on to it, especially early on in training.

Timing plays a very important role, especially with Red dogs.

It is very important to send the message that you are in control with a Red dog. Carrying yourself with confidence is crucial in training this behavior.

Make sure that your voice shows confidence as well. You might find with Red dogs that you need to be a little louder initially.

**O**
**R**
**A**
**N**
**G**
**E**

Orange dogs can be a bit of a challenge at first when you are teaching this behavior. If there is something or someone in another direction that your dog sees as more important than you, he will probably bolt pretty quickly. Always make sure you are prepared for sudden movements.

As you teach your dog this behavior, you will be using a long line. Make sure that you are always holding on to it, especially early on in training.

When you are training your Orange dog, especially as you are beginning to train this behavior, timing plays a very important role.

With Orange dogs, make sure that you always have everything ready as you bring your dog out. It is important for you to demonstrate confidence and preparation when training this behavior.

Your voice is key. You want to make sure that you are very firm in your tone.

**Y**
**E**
**L**
**L**
**O**
**W**

Although this is a mellow dog that is very laid-back in nature, you want to make sure you send a message that this is serious. With the Yellow dog, much of that is in your attitude and voice.

Again, you will be using a long line. Make sure that you are always holding on to it, especially early on in training.

You will find that you don't need to be too loud when calling Yellow dogs.

## REWARDS

It is essential that you reward your dog immediately when he comes to you.

This behavior is nonnegotiable, and your dog needs to understand that this is serious. It's not about getting the treat.

Because this is something the dog must do, the reward will be a tactile reward.

Especially with a Red dog, if there is a fair amount of correcting going on, when he does come to you, kneel down and take some extra time to pet him.

It is essential that you reward your dog immediately when he comes to you.

This behavior is nonnegotiable, and your dog needs to understand that this is serious. It's not about getting the treat.

Because this is something the dog must do, you will use a tactile reward.

With an Orange dog, you may not be correcting your dog as much as you would a Red dog. Even if you correct the dog a few times with the long line and chain collar, it is essential that when your dog does come to you, you kneel down and spend some extra time petting him.

It is essential that you reward your dog immediately when he comes to you.

This behavior is nonnegotiable, and your dog needs to understand that this is serious. It's not about getting the treat.

Because this is something the dog must do, use a tactile reward.

## CORRECTIONS

With the Red dog, you will attach the long line to his chain collar.

The correction will be the pulling of the long line as you tell him to come. The timing of this is very important, and more so with Red dogs because of their high-strung attitudes.

Remember that some Red dogs can be a little hardheaded in the beginning. You might find that at first you have to call or correct your dog a few times before he actually comes to you.

With the Orange dog, you will be attaching the long line to his chain collar.

The correction will be pulling the long line as you tell him to come.

This is another behavior that I have seen Orange dogs catch on to very quickly.

With the Yellow dog, you will be attaching the long line to whatever collar he normally wears. With most Yellow dogs, you do not need a chain collar. If you feel you need it, by all means use it.

The correction will be pulling the long line as you tell him to come.

Remember to make sure that your Yellow dog comes directly to you. As he gets to you, take some extra time to pet and reward him.

# TRAINING YOUR DOG TO COME (Continued)

**MANNERISMS**

**GREEN**

When teaching this behavior with Green dogs, you need to make sure that you show confidence in your mannerisms, but at the same time you want to remember you are dealing with a dog that can be a little hesitant or shy.

Since many of the Green dogs are small dogs, make sure you have a line that is light enough that your dog does not realize he has it on.

The good news is that most Green dogs already look to us for security. Once they understand what you want, teaching them to come to you is pretty easy.

You will find that the tone of your voice does not necessarily need to be loud. Actually, the closer your dog is to Blue, the softer your voice should be.

**BLUE**

There is a fine line to avoid crossing when teaching this behavior to a Blue dog. You need to make sure that you show confidence in your mannerisms, but it is crucial that you do it in a way that does not stress the dog.

There is an art to working with Blue dogs, and teaching the come behavior is a great test.

Like Green dogs, Blue dogs look to us for security. Once they understand what you want, teaching them to come to you is pretty easy.

You can use a soft voice to call a Blue dog.

Before you begin teaching your dog to come, please read these steps:

1. Take your dog to an area with no distractions.
2. Attach the line to the chain collar with Red or Orange dogs. Attach the line to your dog's regular collar with Yellow, Green, or Blue dogs.
3. Hold on to the long line at about the halfway point.
4. Let the dog begin to sniff around and roam.
5. When the dog begins to sniff or roam about 8 to 10 feet away, say your dog's name followed by "come."

| REWARDS | CORRECTIONS |
|---|---|
| It is essential that you reward your dog immediately as he comes to you.<br><br>This behavior is nonnegotiable, and your dog needs to understand that this is serious. It's not about getting the treat.<br><br>Because this is something the dog must do, reward him with petting.<br><br>There should not be a lot of correcting going on at all with a Green dog. If you find yourself correcting him, make sure you reassure him with extra petting time. | With the Green dog, attach the long line to the collar he normally wears.<br><br>The correction will be the pulling of the long line as you tell him to come. Even with a Green dog, the timing of this is very important.<br><br>Remember to make sure that your Green dog comes directly to you. When he gets to you, take some extra time to pet him and reward him. |
| It is essential that you reward your dog immediately when he comes to you.<br><br>Even though you are training a Blue dog, the message that must be sent to your dog is that this behavior is non-negotiable, serious, and not about getting a treat.<br><br>Because this is something the dog must do, the reward will be tactile. | With the Blue dog, attach the long line to the collar he normally wears.<br><br>The correction will be the pulling of the long line as you tell him to come. With Blue dogs, the correction will be nothing more than a very light tug of the leash.<br><br>Remember to make sure that your Blue dog comes directly to you. As he gets to you, lavish him with petting.<br><br>The finished come behavior is another great confidence booster for Blue dogs! |

6. Make sure you say this only one time.
7. Be prepared—your dog may not listen to you initially.
8. If he does not respond to you within the first second, give a quick correction with the leash.
9. He should come to you at this point.
10. As he is coming, guide him in front of you. It doesn't matter whether he sits or stands. All that matters is that he stays in one place, pays attention to you, and does not wander off. Red or Orange dogs are more likely to wander, so be ready to correct.

**Let the dog begin to wander and sniff around.**

11. As he gets to you, give him a tactile reward (such as petting him). Early on in training this behavior with high-strung dogs, I will kneel down and spend a good 20 to 30 seconds rewarding the dog.
12. You want to condition him to accept this tactile reward and look forward to it.

Sometimes Red or Orange dogs will ignore you and be less apt to respond to the correction. If that does happen, you may need to correct the dog a little harder.

## Shaping This Behavior

It is important to convey to your dog that if he does not come to you when you call him, he will be corrected. The corrections are going to vary based on the color of your dog. As your dog consistently comes to you from 10 feet away, start letting out more of the line each time you release him. Let it go 20 to 25 feet, call your dog, and see how he

A direct path is ideal; you should be the focus of your dog's attention.

Make sure that you reel the line in and guide the dog as he is running to you.

responds. If he comes to you after you call just once, you are making great progress!

What you might notice is that after you correct your dog a few times and let him wander, he doesn't want to wander. That's actually a good thing, because he's now beginning to understand what you want. In his mind he knows that he'll still be corrected for wandering. In that situation, you might need someone to help you distract the dog so that you are able to get more distance between you. If a situation does arise in which your dog does not want to leave you, try to spend a lot of time giving a lot of tactile rewards to your dog just to keep things positive.

It doesn't matter how much control you think you have early on; do not take the long line off the dog for at least a week. The biggest mistake many dog owners make is falling into a false sense of security and thinking the dog under-stands what they want when the animal still is learning. You don't want to remove the long line before you're ready: if you call the dog to you without the long line on, and the dog does not come to you, he wins! Not good.

After a while you can start letting the long line slacken some.

Once your dog begins to understand, he will start coming directly to you without your guiding the line.

By taking the long line off too early, you can set yourself and your dog up for some unfortunate results. One of the worst things that can happen is your dog running away or into traffic. From your dog's perspective, because he was not ready to be taken off the long line, he learned that he no longer needed to come to you. In other words, you never had control. Make sure you take it slowly, and do not take your dog off the long line until you know you have the control. The last thing you want your dog to understand is that *he does not have to come to you.*

Chapter

# 14

# Teaching Your Dog the Word *No*

**T**eaching your dog the word *no* is great for many reasons, but the biggest reason is that once your dog understands it, you have an excellent foundation for communicating to him that something is not acceptable. The greatest thing about it is that the dog does not have to be next to you, either. Once he understands *no*, the word works great at long distances, too.

Believe it or not, there are still people out there who will say funny things like, "Don't ever say the word *no* to your dog. He'll think that's his name." You may also have been told not to use *no* because it is not positive. As ridiculous as these pronouncements sound—and there are many others—I have heard them said by self-proclaimed animal behaviorists.

Light long lines work great with small dogs such as this one.

I always go back to the example of a child. Children need to understand right from wrong, and it starts with having an understanding of and respect for the word *no*. In my opinion, any child who does not have that understanding and respect has not received a proper upbringing.

Over the years, such a child has learned that *no* had very little meaning. In the beginning, the parents may have backed up *no* with some sort of correction. But over the course of time, that correction was not consistently used, and the word eventually lost its impact. The same thing happens with animals.

I really like this command because once it is taught and your dog truly understands, you have a great way of communicating with your dog when he is not next to you. In teaching your dog the word *no*, much like the training of the *sit*, *stay*, and *come* commands, you're going to find that the actual technique doesn't change much based on the color of your dog. What *will* change are the ways you act and correct your dog. In the following pages, I will tell you how those two factors vary according to the personality of a dog so you can use the most effective approach for your color dog. Once you have a good grasp of the appropriate mannerisms and corrections, I will show you how to go about teaching the word *no*.

## TEACHING YOURSELF TO TRAIN

To train your dog effectively, you must first learn *how* to train your particular color dog. In other words, you need to train yourself to train. That involves two key factors:

- Your mannerisms (the way you move, talk, and touch)
- Corrections

Take a look at the table on the following pages, and find the material that applies to your dog. Read carefully, and then begin the training.

## TEACHING YOUR DOG THE WORD *NO*

Based on your dog's color, you now know whether or not to use a chain collar. If you are working with an Orange or Red dog, the great thing about introducing the chain collar as early on as you've done is that you've already made the training of the word *no* a lot easier to teach.

- You've already used the chain collar in the pretraining exercise before teaching the *sit* command.
- You've used it in teaching your dog to come to you, too.
- Since the dog understands it, you're not going to need to correct your dog too hard, if at all.

The same thing applies to Yellow, Green, and Blue dogs. Since you have already worked with your dog to come, your dog already knows and understands what having the long line on is like.

The whole idea when you start training this behavior is pairing the word *no* with a light correction. When we pair things, it just means that both will have the same meaning, so *no* and the correction will be equivalent right from the start. Over the course of time, we will eventually phase out the correction and need only say "No."

## MANNERISMS

**R**
**E**
**D**

The one thing you want to remember with a Red dog is that he might not listen initially. You want to be prepared for that right off the bat.

Whenever you say "No," make sure you back it up with the same correction; be consistent.

Your mannerisms should always remain the same, too. The mistake that some people make is getting upset and raising their voices at their dogs. Constantly losing your patience and changing your correction can be seen as reinforcement by your dog.

The anchor principle that I mentioned earlier in this book really applies here. Make sure you stay in one place as you are training your dog for this behavior.

Don't be afraid to be a little loud with the Red dog if you have to. You want your voice to mean something.

**O**
**R**
**A**
**N**
**G**
**E**

Orange dogs may not listen right away, but from what I have seen, after a few corrections, they really start to understand.

As with the Red dog, when you say "No," make sure you back it up with the same correction; be consistent.

I think some people have a tendency to lose their patience, get a little upset, and start raising their voices at Orange dogs. Remember that by constantly losing your patience and changing your correction, you can be reinforcing your dog's actions.

The anchor principle applies: stay in one place as you train your dog for this behavior.

You will find that you can be a little loud with your Orange dog. You always want your voice to mean something.

**Y**
**E**
**L**
**L**
**O**
**W**

Yellow dogs will catch on to this pretty quickly. You may only need to say "No" a few times and back it up with a few corrections, and the dog will understand.

The tone of your voice will be much different than if you were training an Orange or Red dog. You will probably notice with that you will not need to be so loud with a Yellow dog.

## CORRECTIONS

With the Red dog, attach the long line to his chain collar.

The timing of saying the word *no* is very important, especially with Red dogs, because of their high-strung attitude.

Remember that some Red dogs can be a little hardheaded in the beginning. You might find that at first you may have to say "No" and correct him a few times before he actually understands what you want.

With the Orange dog, attach the long line to his chain collar.

The timing of saying "No" is very important with Orange and Red dogs.

An Orange dog still has that high-strung attitude and personality, so remember that you might have to correct him a few times before he actually understands what you want.

Attach the long line to whatever collar the Yellow dog normally wears.

The correction will be very minimal—just a very light tug on the line.

After a few times of correcting your dog, you may find that you do not have to do anything other than just say "No."

# TEACHING YOUR DOG THE WORD *NO* (Continued)

**MANNERISMS**

| | |
|---|---|
| **G R E E N** | You want to be very careful when teaching this behavior to Green dogs. Whenever you train a Green or a Blue dog in anything that involves a bit of correction, you want to make sure things are always kept in a positive direction.<br><br>With Blue and Green dogs, your voice will be a lot softer. That's because these dogs are already sensitive to loud voices. |
| **B L U E** | You want to be very careful with teaching this behavior to Green dogs, and even more careful with Blue dogs. Whenever you train a Green or a Blue dog in anything that involves a bit of correction, you want to make sure things are always kept in a positive direction.<br><br>Your voice will be a lot softer with Blue dogs, almost your normal tone. If this is a very skittish dog, which many Blue dogs are, raising your voice could have a negative impact on your dog. Blue dogs can be very sensitive to loud voices. |

To teach this command, put your dog in a situation in which he has the ability to do something wrong, so that you can correct him. Here are three examples:

- If your dog likes getting in the trash, use that to train him.
- If he likes jumping on people, use that to train him.
- If he likes putting his foot on people as they are eating, use that to train him.

For a Red or Orange dog, you most likely will not have a problem finding something that he does wrong. There are so many other things that you can use to teach *no*, but I think you get the idea. With the Yellow, Green, or Blue dog, you may have to be more creative in setting up your situation.

The tool that you'll need is the same 30-foot long line you used in training the come behavior. Again, if you have a dog smaller than 30 pounds, my suggestion would be to make a line out of something light like a quarter-inch nylon rope.

With the Green dog, attach the long line to the collar he normally wears.

The correction will be very slight, if any. It may be nothing more than a very light tug on the line.

As with the Yellow dog, after a few corrections, you may find that you do not have to do anything other than just say "No."

Attach the long line to the Blue dog's normal collar.

The correction will be ever so slight, if any. It may be nothing more than a very gentle tug on the line.

As with the Yellow dog, after a few corrections, you may not have to do anything other than just say "No."

Again, watch the level of your voice, even when using it as a correction.

Let's use an example of a trash can in the kitchen. Attach the line to the chain collar or your dog's collar, and read this before training your dog on this behavior:

1. To set up the situation for a dog that likes getting into the trash, keep the trash can in its natural place or in an area that the dog is most likely to access.
2. Connect that 30-foot long line to the chain collar or collar. Hold on to the long line at about 15 feet. You are going to go through the same training technique as you did with the come behavior.
3. Keep a lot of slack in the leash. You don't want to telegraph to the dog that you've got a line on him.
4. Let your dog make his way to the trash can, still keeping that slack in the leash.
5. When your dog gets to the trash can and just starts getting into it, say "No" once and give the dog a correction with the line at the *exact* same time.

6. If the dog stops and looks at you, immediately walk over to him and give him a tactile reward. This will let him know that what he just did at that exact moment was correct. In this case, you said "No," you corrected him, and he responded correctly—and it is essential he is rewarded for that.
7. Take him away from the area and spend a few minutes with him, just petting and playing.

Give your dog a 5- to 10-minute break before you try it again. When you do so, repeat what you just did. The only difference is, each time you repeat it, make sure you concentrate on giving a much lighter correction. You should use the same tone of voice you used when you first said "No." With Blue, Green, and Yellow dogs, you may not even use much of a correction at all.

Use a "forbidden" object that your dog finds particularly alluring (such as a trash can) to attract his attention.

You can see that as I say "No" and correct the dog, the dog turns and responds.

As your dog begins to understand the word *no*, you'll find that you'll begin to phase out the physical correction altogether. Once this happens, your dog understands.

The whole idea behind this training exercise is that by using a physical correction combined with the word *no* initially, you let the dog know exactly what you mean.

# CONCLUSION

I look back at some of the teachers whom I have known, and the best ones were always the instructors who could identify students, understand them, and teach them based on their personalities and drives. The same thing applies to animal trainers. The best animal trainers are always the ones who can get to know the animal, develop a great relationship, and *train the animal based on the animal's personality and attitude*. I hope that *What Color Is Your Dog?* has helped you with that!

When I first started writing this book, I knew that it was going to deal with the training of dogs based on personalities. I remembered a dog trainer I knew many years ago who epitomized everything I have been telling you throughout this book.

One of the best dog trainers in the film and television industry was named Frank Inn. Frank was the owner and trainer of the dogs who played Benji. I met Frank on a number of occasions, and he was a very kind man. Frank Inn died in 2002, but his memory will never be forgotten.

I had met the second Benji a few times, and she was definitely a *Green dog*. I know this because one of my best friends, Bryan Renfro, trained her for Frank for the motion picture *Benji the Hunted*.

In my opinion, the reason Frank Inn will go down as one of the top dog trainers in his industry is not simply because he was good. Most significant, he took a Green dog and made her one of the top working animals in movies and television at that time.

As you work with your dog, I am going to ask you to do something as a favor to me. If you learned something from this book, share it with a child, or someone young. We need to teach young children so much about responsible pet ownership and training. I really believe that if enough kids learn at an early and impressionable age, we can make a difference. There will be fewer dogs in animal shelters and humane societies, and more in caring homes with families that love them.

# CREDITS

Training photos courtesy of Tara Gregg. Additional photos courtesy of Gina Cioli and Pamela Hunnicutt/BowTie Inc., Joel Silverman, Evan Cohen, Isabelle Français/BowTie Inc., Tara Darling/BowTie Inc., and iStockphoto.com.

Illustrations by Brent Griffith.

Special thanks to the Irvine Animal Care Center in Irvine, California, for the use of their dogs and their facilities.

Special thanks also to Steve Martin's Working Wildlife.